C1 2 20 22590 D3

D1331980

THE STORIES
BEHIND THE SCENES OF THE
Great Film Epics

THE STORIES BEHIND THE SCENES OF THE

Great Film Epics

by MIKE MUNN

GLASGOW DISTRICT LIBRARIES

ILLUSTRATED PUBLICATIONS
COMPANY LIMITED

GLASGOW DISTRICT COUNCIL — LIBRARIES DEPARTMENT

LIBRARY	DATE REC	£6·95	CLASS
E1	1 8 NOV 1984		791·43

STOCK C1 2 20   22590 D3

© Illustrated Publications
Argus Books Ltd
14 St James Road
Watford
Herts

First Published 1982

ISBN 0 85242 729 8

No part of this work may be reproduced in
any form, by print, photography, microfilm
or any other means without written
permission from the Publisher.

An Illustrated Publications book, produced
by Argus Books Ltd, Watford, on behalf of
The Illustrated Publications Co Ltd 12-18
Paul Street, London, EC2A 4JS.

Filmset by Computer Photoset Ltd
Birmingham

Printed by Graficromo S A Cordoba
Spain

Introduction

This is not an analytical tome, neither is it a critical volume. It is, as the title states, stories from behind the scenes of the great film epics.

Whether or not the term "great" can be applied to all the films mentioned herein is arguable. What I have tried to do is base the work purely on personal preference but with an aim to be as comprehensive as possible. While even I would admit that not every film I have chosen for inclusion might be deemed a great film, I believe that each and every one has some element of grandeur or greatness about it, whether it be evident solely in the making or in the final result.

The exact definition of an *epic* is again debatable. To avoid argument, and to selfishly cater to my own tastes, I have scanned far beyond, and included the more obvious choices like *Ben-Hur* and *Cleopatra*, to include, for instance, war pictures such as *The Longest Day*, westerns like *The Alamo* and even comedies of *The Great Race* mould, but never venturing too far into those territories because they belong to their own genres. The choice of such films is purely on a basis relevant to the term *epic*.

Having got all that out of the way, may I say that no other type of motion picture has ever thrilled me as the *epic* has done. As a child I positively loved the sight of thousands of blood thirsty Roman, or Greek, or Persian soldiers marching to war on a Cinemascope screen. As I grew up I became more discerning, finding entertainment in the dramatic sweep of Ben-Hur's thirst for vengeance against Messala, the spiritual uplift of Moses at the Burning Bush, the emotional sweep of El Cid's love for his bride and his country, but nevertheless I always remained fascinated with pure pageantry and colossal spectacle. Gladiators spilling blood in the arena to the perverse delight of their vast audience, the awesome parting of the Red Sea, John Wayne and a hundred and eighty other heroes defending the Alamo against five thousand Mexican troops, 16th Century Cossacks riding into battle with swinging sabres and flying scalplocks, and of course the thrilling experience of seeing twelve chariots pounding blood, sweat and sand into the great Circus; these are the memories that still haunt me, and I am saddened that filming such scenes is almost now a dead art and my children will only ever see such sights on the tiny, intimate television screen.

How these films of magnitude and spectacle were brought to the screen is often a tale of dedication, tragedy, courage and pure perseverance. Lives have been lost, love has been found and friendships have been formed and broken just over the making of an epic movie. I have determined to compile such stories and the end result, though I fear falling somewhat short of my goal, is a labour of love.

I am indebted to many for their valuable assistance in the compilation of this book; to such creative artists as Charlton Heston, Jesse Lasky Jnr, Carroll Baker, Angela Lansbury, Peter Snell, James Stewart, Robert Powell, Tony Curtis, Glenda Jackson and the many other famous film names who allowed me to question them at length; and to friend and colleague Dave Smith for access to an important interview of his, and for the use of his beautiful and exhaustive collection of illustrations I thank my friend Richard Green.

And if I may be allowed a dedication, this book is for Tony and Lisa and the children who will come after them, and for my dear June who put up with me during the three years I worked on this book.

The Stories Behind The Scenes
of The Great Film Epics

Messala (Francis X. Bushman) thunders around the circus. (Ben-Hur – MGM)

ELDER PARK LIBRARY

BEN-HUR: The classic epic! The book, a best seller. The silent picture, one of the most successful of all pre-talkie films. And the 1959 multi-Oscar winning movie, the greatest film ever made.

By 1905, when General Lew Wallace died, his book "Ben-Hur" had turned into the biggest money-spinning stage production since its first run in 1899. The story of a Judean nobleman imprisoned by his treacherous Roman friend, Messala, inspired film director Sidney Olcott of the Kalem company. So when a chariot race was staged at a fireworks display he saw the opportunity of putting *Ben-Hur* on film. It was a time when the motion picture industry was still teething, and all Olcott had to

do was take along a cameraman and a couple of actors to the track to shoot the race, add a reel of interiors, and *Ben-Hur* made screen history . . . but for all the wrong reasons.

It was released in 1907 when motion-picture rights didn't exist. Even so, the outraged publishers of the book and the producers of the stage production filed a suit against Kalem. Victory didn't come easily. Finally, in 1911, Kalem admitted defeat and withdrew all copies of the film, having lost 25,000 dollars to the winners of the case. As a result, motion-picture rights were introduced, and, when in 1922 the Goldwyn film company wanted to make a legitimate film version, they convinced

the "Ben-Hur" stage producers that theirs was the ideal company to transfer Wallace's story to the screen. They won the rights, but only after agreeing that the figure of Christ, who plays such a vital role in the tale, would *not* be shown.

Goldwyn's head scenarist, June Mathis, went to work on the screen treatment. Being a powerful figure in the company, she had control over choice of cast and director, and she decided to make the film in Italy. Her choice for Ben-Hur was George Walsh; for Messala, Francis X. Bushman, and for director, Charles Brabin.

Bushman, who always played great lovers, was not so sure he should play

7

such a despicable character. He went to William Hart who had played Messala on stage for years.

"Bill, should I play this filthy Roman?" he asked.

"I tell ya, Frank," said Hart, "that's the best goddamned role in the story. Once they got me to play Ben-Hur and it made me sick. I couldn't wait to play Messala again."

The film company assembled in Rome, and that's when it all started to go wrong. Bushman was informed on his arrival that he wouldn't be needed for some weeks yet; June Mathis was told that she would not be allowed to counteract Brabin's decisions, and poor George Walsh, who revelled in the prospects of being promoted from routine actor to superstar, received nothing like the treatment generally accorded a movie star.

Back in Hollywood Goldwyn merged with Metro and Louis B. Mayer. The new group of producers, Irving Thalberg, Mayer and Harry Rapf, viewed Brabin's footage and all agreed it looked *awful*. Brabin was immediately replaced with Fred Niblo and new

Metro star Ramon Novarro became the new Ben-Hur. June Mathis was also replaced . . . by scenarists Bess Meredith and Carey Wilson. Bushman remained. So too did Carmel Mysres as Iras. May McAvoy was cast as Esther and Frank Currier played Quintus Arrius.

Louis B. Mayer made his presence felt in Italy at the worst possible time. Niblo was staging the great sea battle between Roman and pirate forces during which pirate ships had to ram Roman galleys. There would be hand-to-hand fighting and when one of the galleys was set on fire, chosen extras would leap into the sea.

Full-size ships had been built and Italian extras were hired. But many of the extras, having come from poverty-stricken areas and needing the money, had lied about being able to swim. A motorboat towed the pirate ship which crashed into the side of the galley. Some extras panicked and dropped to their knees in prayer. The galley was set alight and all hell broke loose.

The wind blew up and the fire began to spread. Extras poured over the side,

many in full armour. Watching from the shore, Bushman turned to Niblo. "My God," he cried, "Can't you see, they're drowning!"

Many on call that day gave their own differing accounts of what happened and how many had died. But Novarro, who watched with Niblo and Bushman, assured everyone that no-one was killed.

The true figure of any casualties has never been revealed.

Things didn't go too well for Frank Currier. He and Ramon Novarro spent three days at sea shooting the raft scene and both were exposed to bitter winds. Novarro saved Currier from catching pneumonia by slapping him constantly between takes and filling him with brandy.

The film's greatest highlight, the fabulous chariot race, was not without incident. Action director Reaves Eason was given a free reign to shoot the race and his thorough ruthlessness resulted in the deaths of many horses; about a hundred, as Bushman was informed by one of the crew.

Drivers hardly fared better under

(Opposite) Even before the race begins, Ben-Hur (Ramon Novarro) and Messala display their mutual hatred. (Right) Ben-Hur and Tirzah (Kathleen Key) are horrified when a tile falls and strikes the governor. (Bottom) At the height of the race Messala forgets all about sportsmanship? (Ben-Hur—MGM)

Eason's direction in the huge Italian set of the Circus. A stunt man was killed when his chariot wheel broke as he turned one of the spina's corners. The hub hit the ground and the driver was catapulted through the air, landing on a pile of rubble. He died of internal injuries. It was decided that the race track was inadequate and a return to Hollywood was ordered.

The new Circus rose in Culver City, a cunning combination of a full-size spina with lower stands, and a mini-ature showing upper stands. Thousands of extras packed the real stands, among them stars such as Douglas Fairbanks, Mary Pickford, Lillian Gish and Harold Lloyd. Forty-two cameramen surrounded the arena and a number of assistant directors (among them William Wyler who later directed the 1959 master-piece) mingled with the crowd.

Reeves Eason needed only establishing spectacle this day and offered a special bonus to the winning charioteer. The crowd responded and bets were placed. Both crowd and charioteers gave their all for a breathtaking sequence.

Eason spent further weeks in an empty arena working on the compli-cated shots including close-ups of Novarro, Bushman, horses and wheels. On the last day of shooting the chariot-eers and crew assembled in the arena for the last time. All were eager to get the film finished and get home for Christ-mas. At the end of the day the men were exhausted and the horses stood dripping sweat. Suddenly they realised it was all over. Tears were in everyone's eyes as they shook hands and bid their farewells. They couldn't believe their jobs were done having gone through so much.

Ben-Hur was premiered at the George M. Cohan Theatre in New York on December 30, 1925. It was a resounding success. Audiences revelled in the violence as chariots piled up and sailors were decapitated. There was also the religious element. A Technicolored Nativity outraged some, including Fred Niblo who refused all credit for that scene, having left it to Ferdinand Pinney Earle to direct. Niblo did, however, set the effective standard that Wyler later followed, by showing only Christ's hand or shadow in the scenes He featured in.

"I want to get back home but I'm damned if I thought I'd be rowing all the way."

(Above) Charlton Heston puts his back into the role of Ben-Hur. (Above right) Clean shaven and freed from slavery, Ben-Hur enters Rome.
(Right) Ben-Hur joins in the naval battle.
(Ben-Hur — MGM)

A little over thirty years after the premiere of *Ben-Hur* Metro-Goldwyn-Mayer recognised the potential in their screen property if presented in the most modern cinematic techniques then available. MGM envisioned a *Ben-Hur* in Technicolor and wide-screen. It's fortunate they also decided on enlisting the talents of a fine director, a superb cast and marvellous technicians or the film might possibly have ended up nothing more than a screen extrava-ganza rather than a classic worthy of all the eleven Oscars it won.

Charlton Heston was making *The Big Country* for director William Wyler when MGM first approached him about their new *Ben-Hur*. Wyler was going

(*Top*) Messala (Stephen Boyd) sends Ben-Hur to the galleys on a trumped-up charge.
(*Middle*) Sheik Ilderim (Hugh Griffith) reveals his plan to enter in the chariot race.
(*Bottom*) Jack Hawkins, as Quintus Arrius, found the fighting hot work! (Ben-Hur – MGM)

to direct it, which pleased Heston, but he wasn't so sure about the role they were offering – Messala! Wyler assured him that Messala was a challenging role, one that only a superior actor could undertake successfully. Heston wasn't so sure. Probably like Francis Bushman before him, he couldn't quite see himself as a Roman heavy who not only imprisons his best friend on a false charge but can't even compete in a chariot race without cheating.

However, Heston said neither nay nor yea and as 1957 rolled into 1958 even Wyler began to wonder if Heston would be more suitable as Messala or in the title role itself. Originally an Italian actor had been chosen for Ben-Hur but the failure to teach him enough English quickly enough so that he could limp through the role saw to his exit from the project. Finally Wyler decided Heston should play Ben-Hur and when Heston found out, he and his wife Lydia celebrated that evening with the help of a bottle of champagne and the thought of eight months in Italy where, like the silent classic, the picture was to be filmed.

Heston arrived in Rome on April 13 and caused a riot. He was flanked on every side by reporters, and the surrounding crowd, inspired by his performance in *The Ten Commandments* just a couple of years previous, chanted "E Moses! E Moses!" ("It is Moses!")

The following day Heston met the most famous action director of all time, Yakima Canutt, who was to stage the chariot race and get his actors to at least *look* as though they could drive chariots. These first couple of months would be spent learning the various arts Ben-Hur should be skilled in. Besides racing chariots he had to throw a javelin. His first lesson with the javelins ended abruptly when both the "prop" javelins broke.

Just a week later Chuck Heston gave his first solo performance in the chariot . . . . but only because Yak stepped out from behind him as Heston, unaware of his sudden solitude, continued to manoeuvre the chariot in an (almost) straight run. Yak was able to inform Wyler that Heston would need little doubling when the time for shooting came.

(Above left) Jesus (Claude Heater) sees the cruelty of Rome spreading into his home town of Nazareth. (Above right) Messala and Drusus (Terence Longdon) lead the Roman forces through Nazareth. (Right) The dangerous task of filming the stupendous chariot race. (Bottom) Ben-Hur attempts to help the condemned Christ. (Ben-Hur – MGM)

At a luncheon thrown by the film's producer Sam Zimbalist, Heston met for the first time his leading lady, Haya Harareet. She had met William Wyler two years previously at Cannes, as she explains; "We chatted for a little while, and that was all. I met many people, of course, and so did he. I thought no more about it and I supposed that Mr. Wyler had forgotten me."

But he hadn't. Their brief chat had provided Wyler with enough of an impression of the Israeli actress to contact her a year later with an offer to test for the role of Esther.

Heston, when he saw her, seemed impressed also. When Stephen Boyd arrived in Rome to play Messala he and Heston hit it off right away. While the cast seemed happy with each other, they weren't overjoyed with Karl Tunberg's script. Sam Zimbalist and Wyler brought in playwright Gore Vidal to add whatever he could to the mundane dialogue. However, Vidal wasn't giving Wyler what he wanted and another playwright Christopher Fry, arrived in Rome. What was finally transferred to the screen is basically what Tunberg and Fry wrote, but it was Fry's contribution that really gave the screenplay its polish. For instance, when Sheik Ilderim (Hugh Griffith) entertains Ben-Hur, according to Tunberg he said something like, "Didn't you enjoy your dinner?", while Fry changed it to, "Was the food not to your liking?"

(Above left) Quintus Arrius inspects his new galley. (Above) These miniature ships helped win Ben-Hur the Best Special Effects Oscar. (Left) The women in Ben-Hur's life — from left to right; Flavia (Marina Berti), Iras (Kamala Devi whose part was completely cut) and Esther (Haya Harrareet). (Ben-Hur — MGM)

Filming the chariot race proved, naturally, to be as tough as everyone expected it would. Wyler left the spectacular elements up to Yak to shoot. Nobody could have done it better . . . or safer. Yak took his cameras right into the race and casualties were few. However, one member of the MGM publicity department of that time confided to me that one of the chariot teams crashed into a camera and according to him four horses and one man died. (Of course, this is pure hearsay, but very often publicity bods know a lot more than they're allowed to say.)

If racing chariots was exhausting, then for Heston and Boyd arguing was gruelling. Their early scenes together, leading up to their explosive disagreement, gave Stephen Boyd the chance to experience the Wyler touch. Heston already knew it. Wyler made the actors work a lot, while he shot little. And when he did shoot, he would do as many takes as would please him until it was *exactly* right. He pushed Heston through sixteen takes just on one line; "I'm a Jew."

During one day's shooting Heston and Boyd spent much of the day rehearsing a three-minute sequence.

They felt ready to shoot it when Boyd, who had to wear contact lenses to darken his eyes, complained of the discomfort. Three minutes at a time was proving just too long for Boyd to put up with the pain. The scene was abandoned. For some weeks Boyd retired behind dark glasses, a miserable time for an actor who gave his greatest performance in *Ben-Hur*.

Heston and Wyler shot around the Ben-Hur/Messala scenes during which time Heston fell in love (in the story of course) with Miss Harareet and escaped from a prison cell twelve times before Wyler decided the attempt should fail! Heston was refreshed when his scenes with Jack Hawkins as Quintus Arrius began. The sets were totally different and in a sense so was the plot. For Heston it was like starting a whole new picture. Much of the time was spent being chained to an oar as a galley slave. He told Wyler, "I want to get back home, but I'm damned if I thought I'd be rowing all the way!"

For the sea battle, model galleys were used in the long shots. For close-ups of actors, sets were built in the huge water tank in Cinicitta Studios. Hawkins said at the time; "When we were

working under the boiling Italian sun and the temperature was in the 90s, I had to wear almost fifty pounds of armour. How those sailors of ancient Rome ever stood up, much less fought a battle, I'll never know."

On November 4 Sam Zimbalist came to the set and chatted with Heston. An hour later Zimbalist dropped dead in his driveway. (According to a reliable source Wyler agreed to take over as producer, taking an extra 3% of the box office takings on top of whatever else he was getting as director.)

The next day Wyler went before his cast and crew on the set before shooting commenced and gave a brief tribute to Zimbalist. Then it was work as usual. *Nothing* stands in the way of filming a project as immense as *Ben-Hur*.

Script revisions continued, mostly with the help of Christopher Fry. Heston was finding it difficult to understand just what the love story between Ben-Hur and Esther was doing in the film. The fact is, in the book the main love story is between a character called Iras and Ben-Hur, while Esther stands by for a couple of hundred pages admiring Ben-Hur from afar.

In an interview with Charlton Heston he told me, "Iras was in the early version of the screenplay but Willy cut her out. The fact is the love story is really between Messala and Ben-Hur, and their deep boyhood friendship is what the audience cares about. There is no room for either Iras or Esther."

The Great Chariot

Race From Ben-Hur

(*Above*) *Although he loves Esther, his slave, he gives her her freedom as a wedding gift.*
(*Right*) *Christ is crucified on Calvary.*
(Ben-Hur—*MGM*)

(*Below*) *With Esther's help, Ben-Hur takes his leperous mother (Martha Scott) to see Jesus.*
(*Bottom*) *In a stable, Christ is born to Mary (Jose Greci) and Joseph (Laurence Payne).* (Ben-Hur — *MGM*)

During filming Fry complained of the task set before him of including the Esther/Ben-Hur relationship. "If I were writing this as an original screenplay instead of adapting a novel I wouldn't have the girl's role in the story at all," he moaned.

For those who think that making films is just a matter of writing a screenplay and then going out and shooting it, here's news. The unwelcome love scene was finally put together one day in Wyler's trailer with Heston and Miss Harareet doing their bit on the couch and Chris Fry sitting on a desk working out the dialogue as necessary. Well, this is how it started anyway. Less than a month later the scene still wasn't satisfactory and when it was finally filmed Heston did his job like the pro he is, but his heart wasn't in it. (Which just goes to show what a fine actor he is.)

On January 7, 1959 Heston watched as Christ's body was taken down from the cross. Wyler had his camera come in close for Heston's reaction, and when he was satisfied he called, "Cut," and Heston walked away from his last take on *Ben-Hur* in Rome.

As Heston packed his wife Lydia and small son Fraser into the car that would race them for the airport, Wyler caught up with him, shook him by the hand and said with a grin, "Well, thanks for everything, Chuck. I just hope I can give you a better part next time!"

"Tell God that Moses and Aaron are waiting without."

He may have been short, but Cecil B. De Mille towered over his film units.

On January 21, 1959 Charlton Heston was sunning himself on board a ship taking him from Rome to New York when Lydia brought him tragic news. Cecil B. DeMille, the legendary director who had, if indeed anyone had, made a star out of Heston some years previous, was dead.

Cecil Blount DeMille is a name that means as much to the Epic as the name of John Ford does to the Western. His films were legion and in retrospect few were epics. But those few were more than most directors ever made. And his epics are among the most memorable, if not the most critically acclaimed. Fortunately, the public know more about movie entertainment than critics and they revelled in films like *Cleopatra* which had more to do with high camp than history, and *The Ten Commandments* (take your pick which version) which put religion high in the box-office ratings.

DeMille was always a religious man. In many of his movies he cunningly combined religion and sex and yet made it respectable. Although few students of the cinema would readily admit he produced *art*, he knew how to compose striking images with the use of lighting, sets, costumes and camera angles. And no wonder. By the age of ten he used to relish painted masterpieces like "The Prodigal Son," "The Judgement Of Solomon" and "Ruth And Boaz". From such pictures came his inspiration for many sequences in his epics.

His first real spectacle was *Joan The Woman* in 1916. It was the story of Joan of Arc and starred his then most popular leading lady, Geraldine Farrar. His ever-loyal Jeannie Macpherson was given just one week to prepare a scenario while DeMille gave himself just three weeks to prepare the entire film. Despite the lack of time DeMille praised Macpherson for the "splendid work" she was producing. Once production started he shot every day from ten in the morning until seven at night. He dined at eight and then worked on the script from eight until one in the morning. He pushed no-one harder than himself.

To his dismay his leading lady began to prove difficult. She agreed to have the film postponed for two weeks because extra work on pre-production had to be done. But she insisted that they pay her for the lost time. She demanded a staggering ten thousand dollars. DeMille had little choice and submitted to her blackmail.

DeMille was always an innovator. With his cameraman Alvin Wyckoff, he spent weeks developing the largest movie camera ever used up until that time. Its purpose was to shoot in deep focus so that foreground and background objects were equally clear at the same time. It also had a wide-angle lens which produced magnificent panoramas.

DeMille also introduced the telephone for the first time as an aid on a film set. He was in constant contact with his twelve assistant directors who controlled the 14,000 extras used in the battle scene.

DeMille was unable to use Farrar in many of the battle scenes. The actress was terrified of horses and had to be assisted on and off her mount, often in a faint. She had to be rescued by actor Jack Holt when, at the beginning of a charge, she lost complete control and was just able to hang onto her saddle as her horse ran wild. Holt, a fine horseman, chased her across the location and, in true Hollywood fashion, rescued her by catching her horse's reigns and pulling the beast to a halt in the nick of time.

But Farrar did show tremendous courage when preparing for the climax of the film; the burning of Joan. She was tied to the stake and the logs about her feet set on fire. She had been completely covered in a fireproof liquid and she had cotton, soaked in ammonia, stuffed in her nostrils and mouth. The whole experience made her feel sick and when she saw the wooden "stand-in" burn to ashes in the flames she collapsed and was violently ill.

As a tribute to his star DeMille presented Farrar with a mirror carrying a crest of fleur-de-lys, as carried by Joan of Arc into battle.

The film was not received well by a preview audience in New York and DeMille's producer and friend, Jesse Lasky, insisted the film be shortened for general release. Unhappily, the film failed, no doubt due to the heavy criticism the Catholic Church heaped on it.

If DeMille couldn't make a hit out of religion, who could? Maybe at that time people weren't ready for that type of spectacle. D. W. Griffith's towering epic *Intolerance* in 1916 had also flopped. So just imagine the horror that engulfed Paramount chief Adolph Zukor when in the spring of 1923 DeMille entered his office and said, "I want to film the story of Moses. The Exodus!"

Zukor turned red, near to collapse. "Old men wearing tablecloths and beards? Cecil, a picture like that would ruin us. How much will it cost?"

"A million dollars," DeMille answered confidently. "Just think of it. We'll be the first studio in history to open and close the Red Sea."

"Or maybe," replied Zukor, "the first director to open and close Paramount."

DeMille didn't plan to make just a religious spectacle out of *The Ten Commandments*. Half the film would have a contemporary setting. This would be a story of sin to give the picture "mass appeal".

For the location scenes DeMille took an army of actors, extras and technicians to the waste lands of Guadalupe. There a city of tents was erected to house 35,000 people. To ensure morality, a special police force was set up to patrol the camp and prevent men from entering the women's section and vice-versa. The police also rounded up any bootleggers and gamblers who infiltrated the camp.

Only important persons were allowed to enter the DeMille tent with whatever problems plagued them. And even then

there was often a long wait. One day Theodore Roberts in his Moses costume and James Neill who played Aaron stood for an hour outside DeMille's tent waiting for admittance. Finally Neill's patience broke and grabbing someone who was about to enter the tent, bellowed, "Tell God that Moses and Aaron are waiting without!"

Strong winds from the Pacific endlessly whipped up the sand, and actors and extras had to wear veils to protect their make-up. Theodore Roberts, a dedicated cigar smoker, naturally had problems enjoying his favourite pastime with his face covered, so he overcame the problem by cutting a hole in the veil. The sight of Moses dressed in his flowing robes and leaving a trail of black smoke didn't fail to stimulate a reporter's interest.

Not long after, DeMille read a newspaper headline; MOSES SMOKES BLACK CIGARS. He forced the newspaper into the hands of an assistant and ordered, "Tell Moses to cut out that goddam nicotine in public."

For the dangerous task of pursuing fleeing Hebrews, three hundred soldiers of the U.S. Cavalry were hired to drive the chariots. To inspire his actors DeMille had an orchestra stationed

near the line of charge. DeMille's orders to the soldiers were to the point. "Charge like hell after the Israelites!"

A trumpet fanfare signalled the start of the charge. The chariots surged forward at a break-neck pace. Suddenly chariots at the front came too close together and those following turned in every direction. Many chariots overturned and two vehicles, locked together, careered into the orchestra. DeMille loved every minute of it. He

congratulated the injured and used the footage to dramatise the fate of the Egyptians when stopped by the Pillar of Fire.

The highlight of the film was the parting of the Red Sea. DeMille needed to film the Israelites marching in a long column which, when superimposed over the special effects, would make them look like they were passing through the midst of the sea on dry land. To keep them in line and prevent the extras from wandering off course, posts were erected along the route and wire run along them. So the shadows of these posts wouldn't be noticed on film, shooting had to occur at exactly mid-day.

At a quarter to twelve DeMille climbed a camera platform and surveyed the scene. Then he suddenly realised that the land they were about to pass over looked like exactly what it was—a stretch of dry sand, not the bottom of the sea. The minutes were passing uneasily and DeMille knew that if they didn't get the scene in the can in little more than ten minutes time the whole thing would have to be postponed until the next day.

He looked over to the sea and there saw a bed of kelp floating near the shore. He waded in, gathering armfuls of kelp, and suddenly there was a rush of extras and technicians, following his example. In less than ten minutes the kelp was shrewn along the path between the fences and at last it looked like the bottom of the sea.

DeMille again mounted the platform and, at last satisfied, he signalled for action. The orchestra began to play, this time with little fear of being

(Above) The Children of Israel get up to mischief around the Golden Calf. (Right) Moses (Theodore Roberts) is giving his marching orders by Pharoah's son while dad (Charles De Roche) proudly looks on. (The Ten Commandments — Paramount)

*The resurrected Jesus (H. B. Warner)
appears to his disciples.* (The King of Kings
– Paramount)

mown down in a stampede, and the Hebrews moved forward. DeMille looked at his watch. It was exactly 12 o'clock.

The Ten Commandments opened on December 21, 1923 at the George M. Cohan Theatre in New York and it was an instant hit and subsequent box-office success. It had cost 1,475,836 dollars and it grossed 4,168,798 which in the Twenties was a pretty hefty sum to pay for divine laws.

Believing the world was waiting for yet another mighty religious spectacle, DeMille planned to film *The Deluge*, the story of Noah and the flood. But Warner Bros were also planning the same subject and so DeMille set his mind to telling the greatest story ever told, *The King of Kings*. In the summer of 1926 he gave to Jeanie Macpherson a small family Bible and revealed his plans to film the story of Christ.

"This will be the most important assignment of your life," he told her. "I want you to follow the great drama to the letter."

Every member of his staff received copies of the Bible with instructions to memorise every word of the Gospels. His cameraman Peverell Marley was told to study hundreds of biblical paintings to examine how the artists used light effects to achieve their results.

As the sets were erected DeMille grew more and more dissatisfied with them. He finally ended up quarelling with the set designer, Paul Iribe. The arguments became more and more frequent such as when Iribe suggested filming the crucifixion on a real mountain rather than in a studio.

"And how the hell do you get a storm on cue?" bellowed the director.

For the scourging scene Iribe decided to make the set out of hewn stone. DeMille threw the designs on the floor, growling, "Is this your final design?"

"It is," replied Iribe.

"You're damned right it's your final design. Get the hell out of here and don't come back." DeMille turned to Mitchell Leisen and ordered, "*You* will take over the picture right now."

When the cast assembled on the set DeMille called them, not by their real names, but by their characters' names. H. B. Warner was Jesus, Dorothy Cummings became the Virgin Mary, Jacqueline Logan was Mary Magdalene, Rudolph Schildkraut was called Caiaphas and his son Joseph was Judas.

On the second day of filming DeMille invited a group of religious figures

onto the set and proceeded to preach to the converted for seven hours, reciting the entire story of the Gospels. They stood in a semi-circle, guests and cast, while DeMille performed from a pulpit. About the sixth hour there was a cry.

"Who was that?" demanded DeMille.

"It is I, Judas," came the reply. "Please can Jesus sit down? I've been propping him up for the last hour."

Every day H. B. Warner was driven to the set in a closed car and his face was constantly hidden by a veil. The pressure of portraying Christ in this manner caused Warner to return to an old drinking habit. Worse, DeMille learned that a woman had become pregnant and that the prospective father was none other than Warner. Not only was Warner's reputation at stake but so was DeMille's. He sent investigators to learn what they could. In fact they learned a great deal. The woman wasn't pregnant and had never even met Warner. But the fact that such a story had evolved could still scandalise the actor and jeopodise the entire production. The matter was kept so secret that even Warner didn't hear about it until years later.

And it came to pass that the great director D. W. Griffith visited the set while the crucifixion was being shot. DeMille chatted with him, about what only he and Griffith knew, and then suddenly DeMille handed Griffith the megaphone and said, "You shoot this bit." Griffith's contribution was a short sequence showing a group of persecutors at the foot of the cross.

The King of Kings was completed at a cost of 2,265,283 dollars and although it reaped praises from critics

and clergy, it never made much of a profit. The reason for this is not lack of interest on behalf of the public but because the film was loaned out by the Cinema Corporation, with DeMille's blessing, to various religious and charitable groups who paid only a nominal fee to help replace worn prints. However, DeMille was shocked when he learned that the Corporation had performed their own censorship service by cutting out the whole of the first sequence in which Judas meets the scarlet hussy Mary Magdalene. He wants her. She's expensive. He's poor. He sees an opportunity to make some money with some unknowing help from Jesus, thus giving Judas the motive to later betray his Master.

Without this sequence neither the Magdalene character nor Judas make much sense in their actions and DeMille always viewed it unlikely that a man would betray a king "for a lousy 30 pieces of silver."

When sound was introduced to movies some directors, and actors, fell by the wayside. But not DeMille. He made three "talkies" before turning his hand back to his speciality; the epic. It was *The Sign Of The Cross*, a sort of sequel to *The King Of Kings*, with Charles Laughton as the corrupt Roman emperor Nero, Fredrice March as the handsome hero Marcus Superbus (what else?) and the sexy Claudette Colbert as Poppaea, wife of Nero.

Claudette won the role after a long search for an actress by DeMille. After two weeks of production he had still not found his Poppaea. Then one day he saw Claudette Colbert walking by his office.

"Claudette," he called, "how would

you like to play the most wicked woman in the world?"

"I'd *love* it," she replied.

It was 1932 and DeMille hadn't made a film for Paramount, who were producing *The Sign Of The Cross*, for some years. They knew his extravagance and they gave him a restricted budget. Many corners had to be cut. Cameraman Karl Struss used a prism lens to double the size of the crowd of extras, and Nero's palace was by and large a miniature.

Christian clothes and fed to the lions, but the beasts of prey were disinterested. They just stood around lapping up the blood. Trainers climbed into the arena with chairs and whips in an attempt to rouse the lions into an angry appetite. But all to no avail. Finally, DeMille was forced to fake just about every shot.

The film boasted spectacle, violence and sex . . . . plenty of sex. Apart from a near-the-knuckle orgy, there was a naked male slave who accompanied

Nero, implying a homosexual relationship, and even Poppaea had a lesbian handmaiden.

The publicity department had a field day exploiting the more erotic moments and the public responded in the best way. When DeMille's next few less ambitious films failed to equal the success of *The Sign Of The Cross* DeMille began preparations on another sexy epic, *Cleopatra*. Claudette Colbert was a perfect Cleo, of that DeMille had no doubt. But Charles Laughton

But DeMille would be extravagant when the opportunity arose. And arise it did in Poppaea's milk bath. DeMille insisted that actual milk be used, and after Miss Colbert had been bathing in it for two days it began to turn to cheese.

Problems arose with the lions who didn't understand that they were to tear apart every Christian thrown into the arena. Dead lambs were wrapped in

(*Above*) The great feeling DeMille had for religious art is captured in this dramatic scene from The King of Kings (*Paramount*)

(*Right*) Cleopatra (*Claudette Colbert*) gets her man, Antony (*Henry Wilcoxon*).
(*Far right*) Cleopatra bares more than her political whims before the court of Julius Caesar (*Warren William*). (Cleopatra – Paramount)

(*Left*) *Claudette Colbert as the seductive Poppaea in* (The Sign of The Cross — Paramount)

would be a feeble Julius Caesar. Warren William won that role.

The search for a Mark Antony proved a headache. Frederick March would have been ideal, but he was making another film in that winter of 1933. Over Christmas DeMille interviewed many leading men and was satisfied with none of them. In January of 1934 he was waiting to run some tests of young athletes when an impressive deep voice reached his ears. He walked into the room from where the sound came and saw that it was test footage for a film that was to be made. And there on the screen was a handsome, strong definite Mark Antony-type. It was the British actor Henry Wilcoxon. And DeMille wanted him.

They met and DeMille immediately gave Wilcoxon a roaring description of Antony. "He was a man who thought in terms of nations, not individuals. He did and thought things on a grand scale. The world was his canvas."

"Why," said Wilcoxon, "don't you play it?"

This young whippersnapper appealed to DeMille and he and Wilcoxon remained the closest of friends.

Did you hear the one about the actress who showered Cecil B. DeMille with walnuts? It occurred during the making of *Cleopatra*. A ballista (roman catapult) was erected and loaded, not with rocks, but with walnuts. DeMille, from the other side of the set, examined the ballista through his viewfinder. Claudette Colbert's inquisitive nature tempted her (and won) to touch a cord on the catapult. *Twang* went the trigger. *Whoosh* went the catapult. *Rat-a-tat-tat* went the walnuts on De-Mille's bald head.

Again Paramount limited DeMille's budget. Scenes of charging Egyptian chariots during the battle scenes turned out to be the very same that ran down the orchestra in Guadalupe. They were shots from *The Ten Commandments*. Despite the cut-backs DeMille poured a vast amount of the modest budget into the famous barge scene which boasts the most spectacular seduction in the history of the cinema.

Cleopatra stages a massive feast for Antony. A slave girl dances almost naked on a golden bull. Mermaids were chained to the side of the barge. Cleo appears in wispy draperies under which she was completely naked. Dozens upon dozens of rowers strain at the oars to the thunder of the ortators drum beat as Mark falls under Cleo's spell.

C1 2 20   22590 D3

(*Above*) *Angela Lansbury pleased DeMille with her feet.* (*Above right*) *Samson* (*Victor Mature*) *begins the destruction of the pagan temple.*
(*Right*) *Cecil B. DeMille, on the crane, surveys a portion of the full-size Temple set during filming of* Samson And Delilah (*Paramount*)

And then there was Colbert's asp! From the beginning she told DeMille that when the time came to shoot her death scene at the fangs of a snake she would under no circumstances touch the loathsome creature. When the time came he walked up to her with a huge snake coiled about him. She screamed and fled. Then he showed her the tiny asp.

"Oh, that little thing. Give it to me," she cried, and played the scene to the hilt.

DeMille had another winner with *Cleopatra* but he hadn't yet learned, it would seem, that the public were more interested in sex and spectacle than *just* spectacle. His next epic, *The Crusades*, which had Henry Wilcoxon's lionhearted King Richard fighting a Holy war, concentrated more on the action and flopped. The battle scenes were tremendous and the spectacle by and large out-spectacled anything in *The Sign Of The Cross* and *Cleopatra*.

In 1948 he embarked on one of his most profitable ventures, *Samson And Delilah*. (He had originally conceived the filming of the Biblical adventure

This giant set is in fact a miniature, complete with miniature Phillistines. (Samson And Delilah – *Paramount*)

back in 1935 with Henry Wilcoxon as Samson and Miriam Hopkins as Delilah.) However, the Paramount powers including Adolph Zukor who was now 76, weren't convinced that people were interested in Biblical films during this post-war period. DeMille wooed them with a magnificent painting of an almost primeval brute in a loincloth with a sensual, semi-naked girl. This was his interpretation of Samson and Delilah (at least, for the sake of these studios heads). They loved it and gave him their blessing!

Actually, although the combination of Victor Mature as a virile Samson (well, he was, wasn't he?) and the sexiest lady in movies, Hedy Lamarr, as the greatest temptress the world has known, Delilah, made for some pretty hot stuff. The film proved very much a religious experience and *that*

is what really interested DeMille. It was also a very passionate love story and although people always remember it as a tumultuous spectacle, the only really awe-inspiring sequence that gave the special effects department anything to boast about was the climax when Samson brings the house – or to be more precise Temple – down.

Mature entered the film a rather flabby though large figure. It was left to Henry Wilcoxon, who co-starred as the Philistine General Ahtur, to sweat off 30 pounds from Mature in the Paramount gym before a single camera could turn. But even when filming began Mature turned out to be a sufferer of several phobias and his own charm and gentleness transferred themselves uncharacteristically to the camera. During the shooting of the scene where Samson slays a thousand Phili-

stines with the jawbone of an ass, Mature took fright when a wind machine started. He fled to his dressing room and had to be brought back to the set. Over the megaphone DeMille denounced his star for all to hear, calling him a "100 per cent yellow."

DeMille's problems with Hedy Lamarr proved a little less exasperating. She had no real command of the English language and still thought in German, and when before a camera she posed rather than performed.

Playing Delilah's sister Semadar was the blond and beautiful Angela Lansbury who had no real problem in walking off with the film's acting honours along with George Sanders as the Saran. Exactly thirty years after the making of *Samson And Delilah* Miss Lansbury told me of her personal experiences of working for Cecil B. DeMille.

"He was extremely demanding as to what he expected of any performer, whether male or female," she said. "He wanted your total dedication and application to the picture. He took his pictures terribly seriously.

"He had a sort of foot fetish. All the women who worked for him had to wear sandals in those Biblical epics, and so *I* had to wear sandals. He was very anxious to know if you had good feet before he hired you, and I don't think Edith Head (the costume designer) was pulling my leg when she said, '*Don't be surprised if you're asked to come down to his office at some point when the costumes are vaguely ready to show him what we've done and how you look. And don't be surprised if he takes a rather close look at your feet.*' And he did!

"He insisted I was taught to throw a javelin properly so he hired a young man from UCLA to teach me and I could actually throw it damn well before I was through with the picture. I'm sure the men who worked with him would tell you that he used *real* weapons. Henry Wilcoxon used a broad sword in *Samson And Delilah* and it was real and weighed a ton!

"Wilcoxon was a very staunch member of the DeMille team. He was in a number of DeMille's films and DeMille liked him enormously and used him a lot. DeMille was loyal to certain actors. There was an actress called Olive Deering whom he used two or three times in small parts because he liked her so much, even though you barely saw her sometimes on the screen. She happened to be a very good actress.

"That's not God, that's Cecil B. DeMille."

"DeMille was a very old fashioned director and surrounded himself with all the appurtenances of a big sort of mogul-type director. He used to have a man who went around with a chair and was always shoving it behind DeMille whenever he sat down. He also had a man with the megaphone, who was always two steps behind him ready to shove it under DeMille's nose in case he wanted to say something. He would make very loud pronouncements, sometimes quite rude ones about the crowd or maybe a prop man for not having something, so that everybody in the whole stage could hear, which was always rather embarrassing. He certainly cracked the whip.

"He was more concerned with the spectacle than the content or the acting. He really wasn't concerned with the acting. He was only interested in the *attitude* of the people in scenes. And how the scene looked."

Samson And Delilah, the first of DeMille's epics in Technicolor, was exactly what the public wanted, and gave DeMille the encouragement to proceed with his most ambitious project, a new version of *The Ten Commandments* which literally dwarfed all that had gone before.

(*Top*) The sultry couple, Samson and Delilah (*Heddy Lamarr*). (Samson And Delilah — *Paramount*)

(*Right*) The Lord (*Charlton Heston*) tells Moses (also *Charlton Heston*) "Take off thy shoes from off thy feet." (The Ten Commandments — *Paramount*). (*Above*) The other law-giver; DeMille.

(*Opposite*) DeMille literally filled the screen for the fabulous Exodus sequence... and nearly died for it. (The Ten Commandments — *Paramount*)

One of DeMille's closest associates was the writer Jesse Lasky Jr., He was with DeMille for fifteen years and wrote eight of his pictures. He was heavily involved on the script of *The Ten Commandments* along with three others; Aeneas MacKenzie, Jack Gariss and Fredric M. Frank.

More than anyone Mr. Lasky was able to give me a clearer image of DeMille. As a forerunner to the story behind the making of *The Ten Commandments* here is Mr. Lasky's own reminiscences:

"I never in my life called him anything but *Mr. DeMille*, even though I knew him for fifteen years. I loved him, admired him, learned almost everything I know from him, because I went to him as a very young writer on the first version of *The Buccaneer* (1937), although I didn't get a credit. He said to me, '*I'll have you back working for me,*' and he did .... very soon. I wrote the next picture, *Union Pacific.*

"He taught me the most important thing I have ever learned about screen writing. You can write and hold an audience in any scene providing, and I quote DeMille, '*you have a snake under the bed.*' You have got to be able to cut to the snake under the bed. You can have two people sitting there all day

long and discuss the philosophy of whatever as long as you can cut to the snake under the bed. *That* will hold the audience.

"And he taught me to always rely on something visual. For instance, if the Heavy says, '*I think you're riding for trouble*', no matter how brilliantly he says it, it is wasted unless while he is saying it he takes his glass and empties it slowly like blood dripping. I tell you, we went mad trying to think up little things for actors to do with their hands. In those days when a writer wrote a film, he almost directed it on paper."

I asked Jesse Lasky Jr., about DeMille's obsession with everything on the set *except* for the actors. He told me; "Once I walked up to him when we were making *Samson And Delilah* and said, '*Sir, did you hear the way Victor Mature said that line?*' And he said, '*Of course not. Did you see what was at the back of the stage?*' I said, '*No.*' He said, '*One of the Philistines was wearing a wrist watch.*' "

Was DeMille really a very religious man?

"He was very religious, *but* you have to remember that basically he was an *actor*. He would adapt himself to the audience. He suddenly became a Mormon among Mormons, a great Catholic

to the Catholics. He sort of fell into the colour of the setting, and he was the actor who always seemed to become the leading man in whatever company. He was a great performer on and off the set.

"Religion gave him an opportunity to exploit sin by concentrating on the wages. You talk about the wages of sin so you must *show* sin. Well, this makes a very interesting film. If you want to show the ten commandments being delivered from the top of the mountain you have to show the orgy of the golden calf. So he got away with things in films that nobody else could because it was all being done with a religious subject. But he was indeed a religious person. His first question to me was, '*Jesse, do you believe in God?*' I said, '*Yes, sir, I do. But I also believe in you.*' That was the correct thing to say.

"One day, as I was working on the script of *The Ten Commandments*, he came to me and said, '*Jesse, I'm about to write my autobiography.*' Of course, I was thrilled that he was going to undertake such a thing but not for the reasons that anyone might guess. I was thrilled because it meant that he would not be calling me up day and night, hounding me with the fact that I hadn't been able to write a great scene

(Above) Hebrew overseer Dathan (Edward G. Robinson) offers his humble services to Prince Rameses II (Yul Brynner). (Above right) Etheopia offers homage to Pharoah (Cedric Hardwicke), while Prince Nefretiti (Anne Baxter) gives Moses that old come-on look. (The Ten Commandments – Paramount)

for Moses or I hadn't been able to come up with a particular line or piece of business that haunted him. So when I heard he was writing his autobiography I was delighted and said, 'O, you must, you must. — And he said, 'No. Not me. You will write my autobiography.' I said, 'Will I, sir?' He said, 'Yes'. I said, 'How marvellous.' He said, 'I'll tell you what I'm going to do. I'm going to lock you into the library in my house. Day and night, your meals will be brought into you. You will see nobody but me. For hours, day and night I will be in communication with you. We will cut off the telephone. You can see nobody, think of nothing except this tremendous task that we are going to do together.' And as I heard that, my enthusiasm cooled, and I said, 'Sir, I don't feel I'm equal to it. Leave me alone with Moses. He will take all my time and I think it better to stick with him and let a far, far greater writer do the life of DeMille.''

And so Jesse Lasky Jr., escaped that fate, but the writing of The Ten Commandments proved to be a task as immense as just about anything he'd ever undertaken. To create a screen story around the life of Moses that

would run for nearly four hours on the screen, relying on the Bible as a synopsis was out of the question. Explained Lasky, ''There are years of Moses' life that are completely missing and we had to go to all the source material such as Jospehus and Eusebius, and we had various accounts that had been translated for us. We had an enormous research department.''

They also had an enormous cast; Charlton Heston as Moses, Yul Brynner as Rameses, Anne Baxter, Yvonne De Carlo, Edward G. Robinson, Debra Paget, John Derek, Sir Cedric Hardwicke, Nina Foch, Martha Scott, Judith Anderson and Vincent Price. And that's not counting the several thousand extras used and the legions of walk-on performers who were actually credited. Heston's own baby son, Fraser, played the infant Moses, and if you had a sharp eye you would have spotted Clint Walker playing a guard in the Egyptian Court. There was even Woody Strode as the King of Ethiopia. But, out of all these countless names, no-one had been chosen to play the Voice of God.

Lasky recalled to me a discussion between DeMille and his generals as to who should play God.

''We were towards the end of the writing of the script and we had lunch, the three other writers and I, with DeMille. He also had the research men there and Henry Wilcoxon. Whenever we came to a DeMille luncheon we always said to his secretary, 'How's the weather today?' And on this particular day she said, 'Light westerly

breezes, great sunshine, lovely weather.' That meant he was in a good mood. So we felt safe.

''Everything was lighthearted and charming and nobody mentioned the script which was a danger area. And then DeMille's questions began to draw dangerously near to a scene that we were working on, and then came the question that was absolutely loaded. An old DeMille watcher like myself could see it coming, and it was, 'Well, gentlemen, can I help you? Is everything going perfectly well with your writing?' Now, if you answered 'No,' you were in trouble because then he'd say, 'Ah! You don't need me. You can make this film without me. Then let's see the scene that's so perfect that it doesn't need my help.'

''But if you said, 'Yes, sir, we need help,' then you were opening up something that would last all lunchtime and you'd either not get a bite to eat or you'd have indigestion all day.

''Then some brilliant soul – maybe it was me – said, 'Mr. DeMille, there is a question that's been bothering all of us.' 'Yes?' 'Well, sir, who is going to be the Voice of God in the scene of the burning bush?' So he said, 'Well, who would you suggest?' Well, this was very dangerous ground because you knew the two men he loved were Heston and Brynner. Now, Heston was Moses and you couldn't suggest Heston because he'd be talking to himself, and you couldn't suggest Brynner because he was the wicked Pharoah. And it was dangerous to get into actors because you might suggest somebody who

(Above left) *His true identity revealed, Moses is exiled from Egypt by Pharoah.* (Above) *On Mount Nebo, Moses ordains Joshua (John Derek) to lead the people into the Promised Land.* (Left) *"Thou didst blow with thy wind, and the sea did cover them."* (The Ten Commandments — Paramount)

voted for Roosevelt or somebody who'd been a little on the left and since De-Mille was right wing this would have meant sudden death.

"So some genius said, '*Well, sir, there's only one real candidate for the Voice of God. You!*' And he thought for a moment. There was a great silence and those of us who hadn't thought of this quickly joined in, '*O yes, wonderful, nobody else, couldn't be anyone else. Right quality, right mood, perfect voice.*' And then our voices trailed off and he said in a rather sad tone, '*Gentlemen . . . . . no.*' '*O, but why sir?*'

'*No,*' he said. '*You see, my voice is too well known, and it would go round the world and everyone would say; that isn't God, that's Cecil DeMille.*'"

Later, DeMille revealed that the Voice of God would be supplied by an unknown voice, Donald Hayne, De-Mille's political speechwriter, and whether or not the wily old director actually ever intended to really use Hayne nobody can say. But for years Hayne was credited with the Voice of God. In 1978 when I met Jesse Lasky Jr., it came as a shock to him when I told him who really did the Voice. It

was, in fact, Charlton Heston; his voice played back at slow speed, but he had to convince DeMille to let him do it.

The filming began on the slopes of Mount Sinai and Charlton Heston made his first acquaintance with a camel which bore the granite-like figure of Heston up the side of the mountain. Ever since then Heston has hated the beasts.

Heston's first association with De-Mille was on the circus picture, *The Greatest Show On Earth* in 1952. DeMille had spotted Heston at the Paramount Studio. DeMille was with his secretary on steps leading up to his office and Heston was driving towards the studio's gates. Heston saw DeMille watching him, wondered if he should show any sign of recognition since he had never met the director, and then rather hesitantly waved.

DeMille turned to his secretary. "Who was that?" he asked.

"Charlton Heston, star of *Dark City*," she said. "You saw the film and didn't like it."

"No," said DeMille rubbing his chin

(*Left*) *Rameses leads his thousand chariots after the Hebrews.* (*Bottom left*) *Moses returns to his wife Sephora (Yvonne De Carlo) after speaking with God.* (*Bottom right*) *After the death of her son, Queen Nefertiti vows vengeance upon Moses, whom she once loved.* (The Ten Commandments – Paramount)

(*Right*) *A stunning study of Moses with the sacred tablets.* (The Ten Commandments – Paramount)

thoughtfully, "but I liked the way he waved."

Now Heston was an established star but the part of Moses was his most challenging film role to date. And he was in awe of DeMille. He told me; "I found DeMille to be a totally gracious man. He could be very tough. He was hard on assistant directors and prop men and the crew, but with very rare exceptions he was courteous to actors. He would always address the extras as '*Ladies and gentlemen*', and he would go to some pain if he was shooting a picture at the end of the year which required a lot of extras, to shoot such scenes the week before Christmas so they had plenty of work.

"I was very young at the time and he was very old and a formidable figure. I was never intimate with him but he was always kind to me."

The experience of filming on Mount Sinai proved a remarkable one for Heston, though he shied away when I asked him if it was in any way a spiritual experience.

"It's very easy to say; I walked on Mount Sinai and found God," he told me. "I abhor that kind of comment. On the other hand, you can't obviously expose yourself to a man like Moses and remain unmarked. Indeed, you can't walk barefoot on Mount Sinai and be exactly the same. It was certainly an interesting thing to do."

A stickler for perfection and an avid researcher, Heston would use his spare time on the set to become Moses, to explore the man's thinking and recite long passages from the Books of Moses. On one occasion, after he had been doing this fully dressed in the Moses costume, he returned to the set and passed through the Arab extras who murmured, "Moussa! Moussa!" which means, "Moses! Moses!"

Filming the orgy around the golden calf, with semi-naked girls rolling around in frenzied passion and men carrying girls off behind rocks at the foot of Mount Sinai (recreated for this sequence at Paramount Studios), proved to be an exhausting party for the revellers. One tired girl even went to an assistant director and asked, "Who do you have to sleep with around here to get *out* of this picture?"

During this scene Heston appears with the tablets containing the Lord's ten commandments and cries, "Who is on the Lord's side?" With that bit in the can an assistant director called "lunch." Heston started back towards his dressing room where he always ate alone, trying to savour the persona of Moses that still trailed behind him as he went. On the way he passed one of the girls from the orgy who pouted at him and said, "Party pooper!"

Moses rebuked the wicked Hebrews: "You are not worthy to receive God's Ten Commandments.' (Below) Dathan makes the understatement of the year: "You take too much upon yourself, Moses." (The Ten Commandments – Paramount)

Producing and directing such a film the size of *The Ten Commandments* is no easy assignment for anyone, let alone a man in his seventies, as was DeMille. In fact, the film almost cost DeMille his life. While filming the Exodus in Egypt, DeMille one day climbed one hundred and three feet to check a faulty camera perched on one of the giant gates seen in the film. He climbed by way of nothing more than a ladder, and as he reached the top a terrible searing pain suddenly shot through his chest. For a moment he was unable to breathe and his face turned green. Henry Wilcoxon was with him and told him not to attempt to climb down. "How am I going to get down?" shouted the director. "Fly?"

From where only God knows DeMille mustered enough strength to climb down unaided. His doctor, Max Jacobson, was on the set and ordered the protesting patient back to his car and driven to his penthouse for a complete rest. He had suffered a heart attack and Jacobson told him he must abandon the film.

Of that occasion Heston recalled to me, "It happened on a Friday and,

by God, he was back on the set on Monday. It was just incredible to see how he could have done it . . . but he did. And the bulk of the film was still ahead of him."

But DeMille did finish the picture and what a tremendous piece of showmanship it turned out to be. It was DeMille's greatest – and last – success. Before premiering it in New York DeMille insisted on previewing it in Salt Lake City, the Mormon capital where DeMille had many friends. The Paramount powers advised him against this. "The majority of that city are Mormons, devoutly religious people," they said.

"Then if they accept the picture," argued DeMille, "so will everyone else."

The preview was a success, as was the subsequent premiere and blockbusting release of the movie.

DeMille didn't direct again, although he had many plans to do so. His health deteriorated and on January 21, 1959, the day Charlton Heston was sunning himself on the ship bound for New York, DeMille's heart failed him, and he died.

Some profits for prophets

Though many have tried, no single director has ever managed to bring to life the Bible the way DeMille did. The most ambitious undertaking to do so was when Italian movie mogul Dino De Laurentiis decided to film the whole of the Bible in the mid-Sixties. Epics were nothing new to him. In previous years he had produced the staggering *War And Peace* and the moving and beautiful *Barabbas*. But the Bible? It proved impossible, despite his idea to have several directors shooting different segments. In the end it fell to John Huston to film a generous portion of the Book of Genesis, and the film became *The Bible . . . In The Beginning*.

Huston, undeniably a brilliant

(*Right*) Noah (*John Huston*) calls the tune.
(*Below left*) Abel (*Franco Nero*) lays slain by brother Cain (*Richard Harris*)
(*Below Right*) Sarah bids farewell to Isaac (*Alberto Lucantoni*) as he prepares to leave with Father Abraham. (The Bible . . . In The Beginning — 20th Century Fox)

director, shrewdly avoided the pitfalls of emulating DeMille and produced a respectable, simply told though sometimes uneven movie. It was also one of those star-spotting exercises when the audience finds itself murmuring, "Look, isn't that Peter O'Toole as the angel?" Well, it was Peter O'Toole, and there was also Richard Harris as Cain, Stephen Boyd as Nimrod, George C. Scott as Abraham, Ava Gardner as Sarah and even John Huston himself as Noah, narrator and Voice of God. Newcomers Michael Parks and Ulla Bergryd portrayed Adam and Eve. The film also saw the English-speaking debut of the popular Italian actor Franco Nero who played Abel.

It was a brief role for Franco, as he well remembered when he told me, "I didn't speak much English at the time and I had one line of dialogue.

(Right) The animals enter the ark. (Below)
"Who can bend the bow of Nimrod?"
Stephen Boyd can! (Below Right) Abraham
(George C. Scott) leads Isaac into the
wilderness to sacrifice him. (The Bible . . .
In The Beginning – 20th Century Fox)

My agent sent me a very funny note
from America. He'd asked me if I was
in *The Bible* and I'd said, '*Yes, I play
Abel.*' So he invited all his friends to
watch the movie and he told me that
he was looking for me to appear, and
at the moment I came on he said he
sneezed and then he looked back and
I was gone. In a way it was the truth
because we all worked a lot but parts
were cut."

With the exception of the Noah's
Ark sequence the film was lacking

greatly in spectacle. It is generally the
flood that is remembered, a sequence
that promised much temperamental
behaviour, not from the actors, but
from the animals. To ensure the animals
remained in their twos as they paraded
into the Ark, a long ditch was cut into
the ground along the path the animals
would take while their trainers would
walk along the ditch, guiding the beasts
to their sanctuary. But in the end all
Huston had to do was pick up his
flute-type instrument and begin play-

ing, and the animals just instinctively
followed.

The biggest problems were with the
people. John Huston handled some of
them with kid gloves, Ava Gardner
especially. One night she had been on
the town with George C. Scott in Rome
after working together in a scene which
called for both of them to play old
people. Maybe it was the strain of
that working day or some emotional
problem between the two co-stars,
but when Ava returned to her hotel

room she was ready to explode.

Then the phone rang. She snatched
it from the receiver. "Yeah? Who the
hell is it?" she demanded.

"It's John, honey," said the soft
spoken director. "How are you, kid?"

Ava immediately softened. "What's
new, John?" she asked.

Huston explained that he had just
returned from the studio where he'd
been viewing rushes, including that
afternoon's scenes. He congratulated
her on her delicate performance. The

(Above) The first confrontation between the Hebrews and Sodomites leaves Lot (Stewart Granger in mid-river) with a wife (Pier Angeli in his arms). (Left) Robert Aldrich gave Stewart Granger a lot of direction! (Below) Stanley Baker as the Prince of Sodom, plotting against his sister, the Queen. (Sodom And Gomorrah)

last of Ava's anger floated away.

"It was real sweet of you to call me, John," she said.

Huston hung up and continued with the game of poker he was playing with friends from the film. He told them, "So help me, I've never had an affair with Ava, but I love her for being the great performer she is. I had a hunch she needed a friendly word, and I was right."

The Bible was not a terrific success although it was a fine film, flawed only by the final dull episode of Abraham. Even the destruction of Sodom and Gomorrah was nothing more than a big bang in the distance. However, director Robert Aldrich had given those cities of sin a grand send off four years previously in *Sodom And Gomorrah*. It didn't shake up the critics though, not that Aldrich was bothered.

"There are two schools of how you get to be a better director," he says. "One is that you sit and wait for a big break with the big star and the perfect script. On the other hand, I've never been able to believe that you get to be

(Left) Runaway slaves get a roasting in
Sodom. (Bottom left) Stanley Baker finds
the Hebrews more than a match in battle.
(Below right) Stewart Granger and Pier
Angeli had their love scenes greatly
enhanced by Miklos Rozsa's beautiful score.
(Sodom And Gomorrah)

(Opposite) The huge set for Noah's Ark
under construction.

a better director by not directing. I've
always wanted to do a Biblical picture.
I don't regret doing *Sodom And Gomorrah*. We started with nothing but a
title, and we came out a year and a half
later with one of the highest grossing
pictures Rank ever had. Yes, it was
heavily criticised. But the sole object
was to entertain and provide profits –
and that's exactly what it did."

It entertained *me* at least. It was the
closest anyone has ever come to emulating DeMille, complete with all the
awe inspiring corn that the old master
used to provide. One of the film's
high points was its superior musical
score by the brilliant Miklos Rozsa
who by now was well established as the
greatest composer of music for historical and Biblical films, having previously scored *Quo Vadis*, *Ivanhoe*, *King
Of Kings* and his undoubted masterpieces *El Cid* and *Ben-Hur*, the latter
of which brought him an Oscar.

Making the film was no picnic.

Stanley Baker, who played the picture's villain, once said of that production, "It was the most agonising experience of my life. That location! We were in a terrible place called Ouarzazate in Morocco. I tell you, when you weren't being chased by scorpions and horned vipers, you were being eaten up by flies and roasted by the sun."

For many, the extreme conditions proved too much. Rossana Pedesta, who played Lot's daughter, was rushed to Rome with heart trouble. Stewart Granger who starred as Lot, leader of the Hebrews, sprained his back and his blood pressure dropped to eighty. Stanley Baker crushed his finger and had to have an emergency operation in his caravan, and a stunt man broke a leg.

Granger welcomed any visitor to the set by saying, "Welcome to hell."

Aldrich remembers, "All the actors in the film hated me for taking them out there. And I can't blame them. It only grew into an epic after we started, so there were no facilities there. But, if nothing else, it was interesting. One day we found a 9 ft cobra in one of the tents."

The Bible, particularly the Old Testament, has always been an irresistible challenge to film-makers. In 1910 Vita-

phone filmed *The Life Of Moses* in five reels, releasing it in serial form a reel a week. Other early efforts included James Cruze as *Joseph In The Land Of Egypt* in 1914, and, in that same year, Universal's outstanding picture *Samson* with J. Warren Kerrigan in the title role.

In 1924 Hungarian born director Michael Curtiz filmed his version of Moses' story in *Moon Of Israel*, produced in his home land. By 1928 Curtiz was in Hollywood where he made the last of the silent epics, *Noah's Ark* for Warner Bros. Darryl F. Zanuck wrote and produced the film which provided probably the most spectacular special effects of the silent era with the portrayal of the great flood. Tons of water cascaded down onto the gigantic sets and at least four extras drowned.

There have been many filmed episodes from the Old Testament made since the advent of sound, not all of which could in any way be termed great, though some are worth mentioning if only to illustrate the endless possibilities the Bible offers. In 1960 for instance Joan Collins (having not yet met her *Stud*) and Richard Egan (a sort of poor man's Charlton Heston) were *Esther And The King*. The saga of

King David has been well, though often ineptly, documented such as in *A Story Of David*, notable mainly for its brave casting of Jeff Chandler in the title-role. It was filmed partly in the Holy Land and co-starred Peter Arne, Barbara Shelley, David Knight and Donald Pleasence. Orson Welles somehow got involved with an Italian production of *David And Goliath*, though not as David nor Goliath, and in 1952 Gregory Peck and Susan Howard starred in the respectable but not overwhelming *David And Bathsheba*.

As a sort of sequel to all these comes the ill-fated mammoth production of *Solomon And Sheba* in 1959. The film was a lavish vehicle for its star Tyrone Power as Solomon, son of King David and chosen heir to the throne of Israel. George Sanders was superbly suave and heartless as the envious brother, Adonijah, while the gorgeous frame of Gina Lollobrigida amply filled the Queen of Sheba's shimmies.

Director King Vidor took his cast and crew to Spain where they occupied much of Sevilla Studios, just outside of Madrid. Filming took them well into a cold November of that year, 1958, when the bulk of the film was then behind them. On November 15, while

(*Above*) *Gregory Peck as King David in* David and Bathsheba.

(*Top right*) *Tyrone Power, sporting his* Solomon and Sheba *beard, on his way to film in Spain.*

(*Right*) *Jeff Chandler portrayed the shepherd king in* A Story of David.

preparing for a duel scene between himself and George Sanders, Tyrone Power complained to his personal make-up man Ray Sebastian that he didn't feel well, but brushed aside any idea of going back to bed.

Just a week before Power had suffered an attack of dysentery which had left him feeling weak. As Power and Sanders rehearsed their scene, during which Power had to fall to the ground and twist to avoid his opponent's knife. Power was clearly showing the strain, and it soon became apparent that he was not up to completing the scene. They called a halt and he retired to his trailer, complaining of chest pains. Later, Ray Sebastian looked in on him and found he had collapsed.

Sebastian raced to find the producer, Ted Richmond, who immediately came to the trailer. As he held Power's hands Richmond began to feel the grip getting stronger as the pain wracked the actor's body. Then Power's eyes closed and the vice-like grip slackened.

He was placed in Gina Lollobrigida's sports car and raced to hospital. But when they reached their destination, Tyrone Power, still in the Israelite robes of King Solomon, was dead.

While the film-world mourned, Ted Richmond was faced with an agonising problem. Do they scrap the whole film or reshoot everything? He decided to press on and re-cast Solomon.

Yul Brynner, so dynamic in *The King And I* and *The Ten Commandments*, was chosen to be the new wise ruler of Israel. He asked for, and was granted, a private showing of everything Tyrone Power was in. The footage ran for three hours, a million pounds worth of film. Brynner announced that he would do it *his* way. At his request extra writers were brought in to compose dialogue suitable for Brynner's own bold style of acting, and new

costumes were designed.

On his first day of filming Brynner stepped onto the set and faced a nervous, still mournful Gina Lollobrigida. Then Brynner held both her hands, smiled, and won La Lollo's confidence.

Recasting Power's role was a bold stroke on behalf of Ted Richmond, and although few have seen the original footage, Brynner's Solomon was the foundation of the movie. The picture itself was a poor, though never dull, imitation of DeMille and is flawed heavily by its terrible ending with an overawed Queen of Sheba finding her cuts and bruises, inflicted by the Israelites, miraculously removed by Jehovah in the ruins of the Temple.

In more recent years few have attempted to return to the pages of the Old Testament for inspiration. But in 1973 Lew Grade spent nearly three

(Top) King David (Finlay Currie) names Solomon (Yul Brynner) as his heir in preference to Adonihah (George Sanders) (Right) The Queen of Sheba (Gina Lollobrigida) leads her people in a pagan ritual. (Solomon And Sheba – United Artists)

million pounds on *Moses – The Law-giver*, made as a television series and released in many countries as a two and a half hour feature.

Burt Lancaster played the title role and gave one of his finest ever performances. Being a self-confessed atheist, Lancaster seemed at first an unlikely choice for one of the Bible's greatest heroes and prophets.

He wasn't bothered about the religious aspect. He says, "This is such a beautiful story, and Anthony Burgess has done a superb job with the script. But don't look for a DeMille spectacle. Our interpretation of Moses is a more human approach. It's a moving story about how the Jewish laws and faith emerged out of a need to survive."

Lancaster's own son, William, portrayed Moses in his earlier days, although it must be said that, although this may have seemed inspired casting, William Lancaster looks nothing like his father.

It was an Italian co-production and much of the cast and the director were supplied by the Italian producer Vincenzo Labella. Among the better known faces in the film were Anthony Quale as Aaron and Irene Pappas as Zipporah Although non-English actors all spoke their lines in English, ITC unwisely had English actors dub over their voices (a mistake they also made later with *Jesus Of Nazareth*).

(Right) Burt Lancaster as Moses. (Below) Moses remains silent while Aaron (Anthony Quale) puts his case before Pharoah. (Moses – The Lawgiver – ITC)

Having been filmed in Israel, Israeli technicians and extras were also used. However, when the Yom Kippur war broke out in 1973 production had to be halted as Israeli members of the unit raced off to fight and everyone else had to be evacuated.

The parting of the Red Sea, always a good crowd pleaser if you can slip it into your film somewhere, was filmed at Sharm el Sheikh. Explains Lancaster, "There was a bank just below the water surface, and through

film trickery I merely got my ankles wet." No doubt, so did the pursuing Egyptians, so obvious was it that the Children of Israel were pacing up the beach as opposed to going through the midst of the waters on dry land.

One of the film's co-stars, Israeli actor Aharon Ipale, who played Joshua, was in London just prior to the film's premiere, and I went along to see him. He hadn't yet seen the film but was going to that day. He told me, "Our film is almost like a semi-documentary,

"They dropped to their knees and made the sign of the cross as I passed."

Jeffrey Hunter as Jesus in King of Kings *(Bronston/MGM)*

whereas *The Ten Commandments*, for me at least, was too colourful. Clothes in those days were very dull, so our wardrobe was made from pieces of cloth that melted into the background. The colours were the same as the ground and the mountains.

"The whole style and script was different from *The Ten Commandments*. In *Moses* you don't see Burt Lancaster coming from the mountain with a glorious white beard which wasn't there five minutes ago."

I asked him if, being a Jew, he saw *Moses* as being a religious or historical character.

"Both," he answered. "I was brought up with a religious background, so I believe in Moses, although I'm not fanatically religious. It's more like a tradition to me, and because I was taught about these things as a child it's comfortable for me to believe in them. But I don't have to believe in someone to play him. Burt Lancaster is an atheist and yet he was able to play Moses *and* the Voice of God. We got on very well and talked about this a lot."

If for nothing else, Aharon will remember *Moses* as being the film that could have ended his career . . . and life. He told me, "In my very first shot in the film you see me having a fight with three or four toughies who all have clubs except for the biggest fellow. I can't remember exactly how it happened, but somehow we misjudged things and the big man really hit me. The blow was so powerful I was knocked unconscious. If he had had been holding a club it would have been my last day of filming."

Aharon told me he was later going to see the film for the first time. I didn't have the heart to tell him that his already well-spoken voice had come under the shadow of the over-obsessed dubbing director.

Despite the seemingly inexhaustible wealth of material to be found in the Bible, there is one particular story that has been told over and over again in many different ways – the greatest story ever told itself; that of Jesus Christ.

As early as 1912 the Thanhouser production company included among their star line-up of movies *The Star Of Bethlehem*. The following year Kalem released their own version, *From The Manger To The Cross*, an unimaginative affair by today's standards with a resurrected Christ flying up to Heaven on great wings, but in 1912 it was considered very daring to show a man portraying the Lord. Both films were more than pale in comparison to DeMille's *The King Of Kings* which, for more than thirty years, remained the only feature film made solely about the Christ.

Attempts during the years that fol- lowed to build films around the figure of Jesus included *Salome* and *The Robe*, in which Jesus remained firmly in the background. Film-makers, it seemed, were not yet courageous enough to present a starring vehicle for our Lord in which He is not only seen but heard also. In both *The Robe* and *Ben-Hur*, for instance, Christ is seen only from behind or the side or wherever, but never so His face is in view. It took a brave producer, a true showman, to make the first all talking picture of Jesus – Samuel Bronston.

led to the eventual fulfilment of filming *King Of Kings*.

With his script written by Philip Yordon, Bronston consulted many religious scholars and representatives from many different faiths. His earlier involvement with the Vatican was no doubt instrumental in prompting Pope John XXIII to grant Bronston an audience to discuss the script.

Cameras began turning on April 24, 1960 in the new Temple re-creation. Nicholas Ray was directing and his impressive cast included Jeffrey Hunter as Jesus, Siobhan McKenna as Mary, Hurd Hatfield as Pontius Pilate, Ron Randell as Lucius the Centurian, Robert Ryan as John the Baptist, Viveca Lindfors as Claudia, Rita Gam as Herodias, Carmen Sevilla as Mary Magdalene, Brigid Bazlen as Salome, Rip Torn as Judas and Harry Guardino as Barabbas.

(Above) General Pompey conquers Jerusalem. (Right) Antipas (Frank Thring) refuses to aid his dying father, King Herod (Gregoir Aslan).

(Opposite top) Antipas drools over Salome (Brigid Bazlen) while Pilate (Hurd Hatfield) simply admires. (King of Kings – Bronston – MGM)

Samuel Bronston was asleep in his home in Madrid when the phone rang. Outside a terrifying hurricane was battering Spain. It was the Sevilla Studio, where Bronston's *King Of Kings* was in production, calling with disastrous news. ''The Temple is being destroyed by the hurricane.''

Bronston didn't waste time dressing. He threw an overcoat over his pyjamas and raced to the studio. There he found his giant set of the Temple of Judea rocking under the weight of the storm. Hundred feet high columns swayed in the monstrous winds, and for the rest of the night Bronston personally directed emergency crews which struggled to save the gigantic construction. But the hurricane won and the Temple crashed into pieces.

It had taken many months to build and had cost a fortune. For Bronston it was the symbol of his dream – to film the life story of Jesus. Finally, there was nothing left standing. Bronston turned to the defeated workmen.

''Rebuild it,'' he ordered, and left. It took three months to resurrect.

Samuel Bronston is a man who has been abandoned by the film industry. His films were excessive in cost, length and stature, but that was because he was a *showman*, and there is little room for such men these days. His career in films began as a salesman with MGM in Paris. He went to Holly-

wood and became a producer with such films as *Martin Eden* and *Walk In The Sun*. The thirst for complete independence in filming prompted him to launch his own company in Spain, and there he produced a star-studded adventure, *John Paul Jones*, just a slight taste of things to come.

Some years before entering the film industry the Russian-born Bronston retreated into a Jesuit hideaway in Italy for physical and spiritual refreshment. Because of his knowledge of art and his skill in photography he became active in preserving religious antiquities. This brought him to the attention of the Vatican, and for several years he devoted himself to the filming in colour of the Holy See's treasure of paintings, sculpture and relics. This

For Jeff Hunter it was the crowning achievement of his career and when he died from a fall in 1967 obituaries were incomplete without a mention of his performance as Christ. His portrayal did not please critics, but then what do critics know what it takes to portray the Son of God? Given what was very much limited space for such a part (the film was really about the life and *times* of Christ, not just about the Man), Hunter excelled. However, it was a story-book Jesus on the screen, but the visual aspect was what Samuel Bronston and Nicholas Ray searched for.

''I really chose him for his eyes,'' explains Bronston. ''It was important that the man playing Christ should have memorable eyes. This film was a

great responsibility. We did not permit Hunter to be interviewed or photographed because the part had to be approached in a reverent manner.

"Jeff took the part very seriously. He had great presence. If he walked into a room in the robes of Jesus you would stand up. I know that at the time it was unusual for Christ to be seen and to speak in a film. But we were making the life of Christ and presenting him as a human being."

Nick Ray had previously directed Hunter in *The True Story Of Jesse James* and recalled, "Although Jeffrey was not playing the principal role, I found myself wanting to spend more time with his performance. I noticed then a quality of genuine gentleness in his conduct with people, and I remembered *that* when we first began discussing the role of Jesus. In Jeffrey was an honest warmth which came across on the screen. I think he was superb as Christ. And above all he had remarkable eyes. You notice them from the first, as indeed you must have done with Christ. That is the feature that I tried to emphasize."

At the time of production Hunter remarked, "I could only approach this role with two guideposts – absolute humility and a willingness to accept emotional and spiritual guidance."

As filming progressed Hunter began to notice the effect of his presence upon other members of the unit. "At first, there seemed to be a timidity, then almost a withdrawal from the usual banter and fun-making on the set. Seldom did anyone engage me in personal conversation. I made a point not to smoke, or appear in any way undignified. This wasn't really an effort on my part. It just seemed right. After a while I would simply go to my dressing room and stay there, studying my lines, until the next scene was ready."

Among the visitors to the set was Joseph Vogel, the head of MGM. What he saw impressed him enough to draw up a deal with Bronston to distribute *King Of Kings*, confusing the film as another *Ben-Hur*. How wrong he was, though *King Of Kings* did have a generous amount of action and spectacle. There were two large-scale battles fought between the Zealots of Barabbas and the Romans. 2,500

extras brandishing swords and spears were unleashed in the giant Fortress Antonia as Barabbas leads the revolt in Jersusalem. Anthony Bevin, an authority on Roman military and author of "The Roman Army In Britain" and "The Formation of the Roman Army", supervised the Roman manoeuvres which culminates in the Phalanx, a wall of Roman soldiers that mercilessly mows down almost the entire Zealot army.

One particular stunt-man made the headlines when he made a 51 ft fall from the Temple. He was Manolo Gonzales, a chunky 5 ft. 1 inch Spaniard who had also performed much derring-do in *Spartacus*, *Solomon And Sheba* and *John Paul Jones*. Gonzales' fall from the Temple was broken only by a pile of pasteboard cartons. He survived the fall with only a few minor bruises and was warmly applauded by a thousand members of the cast and crew who gathered to watch the daring stunt. He was paid 7,000 pesetas, thought then to be the highest price ever paid for a stunt in Spain. With the money he planned to buy his bride of less than a year a baby-carriage for their first baby, anticipated the following month.

The largest scene was, surprisingly, not an action sequence. It was the moving Sermon on the Mount. Some 7,000 extras were gathered against the vista of the Chinchon Hills to play those who heard Christ's words. To follow Hunter's movements down the hill, 300 feet of camera track had to be laid, but because the slope was so steep, and the Super Technirama cameras so heavy, an equal amount of track had to be laid down the other side of the hill along which rolled a weight, equal to that of the camera to which it was connected.

The extras, all Spanish locals and many of them pious, were moved by Hunter's first appearance on the mountain top. Many wept and Hunter began to realise fully the responsibility he had undertaken.

"To my astonishment," he recalled, "quite a few dropped to their knees and made the sign of the cross as I passed by. They knew perfectly well that I was merely an actor playing a part. Still, I was a living representation to them of a figure they had regarded since childhood with most sacred awe. I didn't know what to do, but instinctively pretended not to notice rather than intrude upon this gesture of devotion."

To score the film was the multi-Oscar winner Miklos Rozsa who has made the genre of epic film music his own. He was employed to work on the film from its early stages, a rare experience for any composer, and Dr.

(Opposite top) Jesus staggers under the weight of the cross. (Bottom left) Judas (Rip Torn) conspires with the rebel leader Barabbas (Harry Guardino). (Bottom right) Imprisoned, John the Baptist (Robert Ryan) tries to send a message to Jesus through Lucius (Ron Randell). (King of Kings—Bronston-MGM)

Rozsa spent much of his time on the set. His first assignment was to score Salome's sensuous dance, and his first days were spent watching the lovely 16-year-old Brigid Bazlen writhing about to choreographer Betty Ray's (wife of Nicholas) instructions, not an altogether unpleasant task for the eminent Rozsa. In all Rozsa spent 6 months composing and recording his music for the film which contributed to a large extent to the quality of the finished movie.

When *King Of Kings* was finally in the can another film company came to Bronston with an offer to rent his massive Temple set.

"It served its purpose," he said, "served it well. No, I cannot allow it to be used in any other picture."

He turned to his aides. "Tear it down," he ordered, and then after a pause he added, "But wait until I've left town. I don't want to be here when it falls."

Curiously the film did not fare well at the box office and a very limited re-issue in the early Seventies did nothing to boost its takings. However, when the movie was shown on British TV in 1978 the press actually praised it as well as Jeffrey Hunter's performance and viewers actually sat, watched and enjoyed it.

Whether it was because MGM felt the film was overlong or just slow (the former being the more likely) the picture was heavily cut and the whole of Richard Johnson's performance as David, a Jew who's become Romanised, disappeared. But he does appear fleetingly during the scene when Jesus enters Jerusalem on a donkey. He dismounts at the foot of the Temple and meets David's gaze.

What *King Of Kings* did do was to break the ice concerning the filming of Christ and in 1962 George Stevens began his mammoth Cinerama masterpiece (dare I say? I dare!) *The Greatest Story Ever Told*.

(Above) Richard Johnson's role of David, a wealthy Judean who returns home from Rome, was completely cut out. (Left) Mary Magdalene (Carmen Sevilla) sees the resurrected Christ. (King of Kings — Bronston-MGM)

"If the Jordon had been as cold as the Colorado, Christianity would never have gotten off the ground."

Stevens said at the time that he had wanted to make a film in Cinerama since he first saw the process 10 years previously. "I particularly wanted to try intimate close-ups on the immense, high and wide screen," he once said.

Before filming, Stevens took some colour make-up tests of Swedish actor Max Von Sydow who was to play Jesus which were shown to the press in New York on the Cinerama screen.

Cinerama president Nicholas Reisini felt, "You get the sensation of being behind the eyes of the man, looking into his soul. That's the effect Stevens was seeking with Cinerama, and he has succeeded beyond all expectations."

In fact, Stevens, taking advantage of the newly developed one-lens Cinerama system, (whereas before a camera with three lenses was needed) made one of the most effective Cinerama showcases ever without filming a single battle, chariot race or runaway wagon. He literally swept the audience into the story and gave us the nearest thing so far to the definitive screen Christ.

Over the past fifteen years since the film's release, it has become popular to knock the picture, especially for its starry cast which reads more like a Who's Who. To mention just some of the names there was Charlton Heston excelling as John the Baptist, David McCallum as Judas, Jose Ferrer as Herod Antipas, Telly Savalas as Pontius Pilate, Dorothy McGuire as Mary, Gary Raymond as Peter, Donald Pleasence as the Devil, Joanna Dunham as Mary Magdalene, and in other roles, Van Heflin, Ed Wyn, Shelley Winters, Carroll Baker, Pat Boone, Sidney Poitier and John Wayne as the Centurian. Hardly a single review got past without sóme remark about Wayne's contribution, generally of a derogatory nature. It's unfortunate that many people are narrow-minded enough not to be able to see Wayne in such a role. After all, who better than John Wayne to play a man in authority?

Enough of the gripes against those who griped first of all. The background to the making of the film is full of incident. I'll deal first with the wherefores and later with the whys.

To make the film George Stevens and his associate Carl Sandberg formed a special company and raised their own capital. Cinerama put up a certain amount of the budget, but much of it was paid for by United Artists. For reasons we shall discover later the film was shot in Utah, but not for the reasons given in the publicity handouts in which it was stated that the Holy Land was no longer the landscape it was nearly two thousand years ago.

What follows is a typical day in the making of *The Greatest Story Ever Told*. It's 7.30 in the morning. As the twelve Apostles stride across the Utah desert onto the set, a platoon of Navajo Indians are trying desperately to march like Roman soldiers. Max Von Sydow leaves his bungalow, carrying sandals and a copy of the book *Hawaii*, the film version of which he will star in later. All gather before the walls of Jerusalem, re-created at a cost of 115,000 dollars.

George Stevens surveys the multitude and booms over a microphone, "Good morning, folks. Let's make this a good scene. You're seeing the Lord Jesus for the first time. He's mounted on a donkey and riding into Jerusalem. Your faces must show wonder and awe."

(Below) Jesus (Max Von Sydow) and his disciples rest at the house of Lazarus. (Opposite) In the unlikely setting of Utah, Max Von Sydow and hundreds of actors and extras re-enact Jesus' triumphant ride towards Jerusalem. (The Greatest Story Ever Told – United Artists)

A Navajo Indian interprets Stevens' words for the benefit of the 550 Indian extras.

"Camelpokes, commence to poke your camels on Action. All right folks, show awe. Hosanna! This is the Lord. Haaaaaalelujah!"

Max Von Sydow, mounted on the donkey, begins to ride forward, followed by his Apostles until the multitude threatens to engulf him, filled with the fervour of their director.

"Cut," cries Stevens. "Very good,

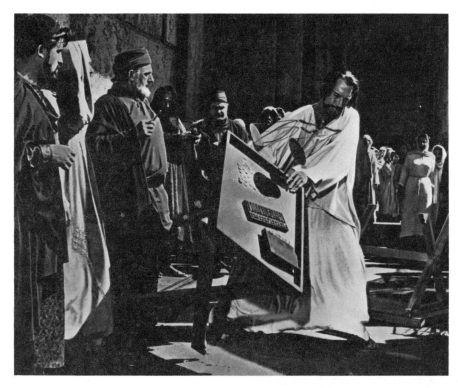

folks. Now let's try it again."

As on *King Of Kings* (both versions) there was a clampdown on publicity regarding the leading actor. Max Von Sydow could not be photographed nor interviewed. Between shots he would sit by himself away from others reading books on theology.

George Stevens was one of those directors who never hurried himself when filming. He spent three weeks just shooting the scenes with Charlton Heston as John the Baptist. That was in a very cold 1962 November spent almost entirely in and around the Colorado River. Heston had been allowed time off from *55 Days At Peking* to play the Baptist. In an interview

(Opposite top) The awesome Crucifixion movingly presented by George Stevens. (Bottom left) Jesus is engulfed by the multitude on the first Palm Sunday. (Bottom right) Charlton Heston baptises Von Sydow in the Colorado! (The Greatest Story Ever Told – United Artists)

with him I asked why he chose to play another Biblical hero.

"Primarily to work with Stevens," he answered. "It was a very good part, too. I think out of all those parts, Jesus aside – and Jesus is really unplayable; if Max Von Sydow couldn't win people's hearts, why then, nobody can – the Baptist was really one of the best. All that lovely stuff screaming about the mountains shall be brought low.

"I must say, baptising Max was a

painful experience. He's a lovely man and a marvellous actor, and I loved playing the scene with him. But we shot down in the Colorado River in November and that bloody water was an average temperature of 42 degrees, and that is *cold!* I was standing up to my waist in it all day long, dipping people. We used a lot of local people to play the baptisees, and George shot quite slowly and meticulously. Often they'd be waiting all day long for their chance to be baptised and they were looking forward to being in a scene. It was lovely to see when it finally came to their turn. They'd step into the water and you'd see this expression of what I trust came across as ecstasy on their faces. And when I would actually dip them under they'd come up semi-conscious. As I said to George at the time, 'George, *if the Jordan had been as cold as the Colorado, Christianity would never have gotten off the ground.*'"

One day, to Chuck Heston's total surprise, Stevens gave the scene in which the Baptist is arrested by Herod's men, to Chuck to direct.

"That was a heady feeling," said Heston, "to have George Stevens say, '*I really have to get back to the studio. You direct this scene.*' God knows, it was a simple enough scene."

(Left) "My house shall be called a House of Prayer – but you have made it a den of thieves." (Below) John Wayne as the Centurion accompanies Jesus on His final journey. (The Greatest Story Ever Told – United Artists)

Chuck remembers the film as being one of the most miserable experiences, location wise, yet a satisfying one. Donald Pleasence, on the other hand, just found it miserable. He told me, "It was a curiously embarrassing experience in a curiously embarrassing film. It was interesting though because it was my first experience of Hollywood. I spent three months on the film, which must have been three months less than the rest of the cast. I think I worked for twenty days. I got to see the whole of the west of America. I used to call the office and say, '*Do you mind if I go to the Grand Canyon?*' They'd say, '*Sure, just call in every night.*' I'd go everywhere I could, or otherwise I'd sit by my swimming pool at my rented *palace.*"

As schedules went way over, United Artists began to worry. It was Christmas and Lazarus still hadn't been raised from the dead after three weeks work on the scene. After the Christmas holidays work continued on the Palm Sunday sequence, but only after the snow had been cleared. While digging, two of the Apostles strained muscles and then the Indians disappeared into the desert to vote in a tribal election. More snow was forecast and on January 9, 1963, Stevens and his unit fled back to California.

In Los Angeles plans were made to save on the budget. At least one assistant director went, certain actors had their parts cut from the script and Stevens was forced to film the Sermon on the Mount in three days instead of three weeks.

The picture was finally completed on July 31 in Culver City, California, where they filmed the crucifixion on a Calvary constructed in the studio. Strangely enough, this proved highly effective and is by far the most moving, powerful and memorable of all the filmed Crucifixions. But how come half of Hollywood suddenly turned up in the final sequences? And just why did Stevens foolishly use Utah as the Holy Land? Carroll Baker supplied me with the answers at her London home.

"Unfortunately there were too many compromises which George made. He made them all with the best of intentions. I think he wanted this film to be the highlight of his career. At that time Hollywood was beginning to be very hard pressed for films. Very little money was generally being spent. George wanted to film the whole thing in Israel and I think it definitely should have been. There is a magic in Bethlehem; the lighting and the mountains there. To have actually gone to the authentic locations would have made a big difference in the film.

"The movie industry begged him not to; to give the work to the people in Hollywood. Besides, the unions then knew they had a big picture and they really came down hard on him. It was a very strong union in America so there was nothing else to be done.

"They said, '*We'll be spending a lot of money on this so we don't want to get in wrong with the Catholic Church.*' Well, whenever you bring in a censor from the very beginning on an artistic project you run into trouble, because part of the criticism was that some things were done too literally.

"Then the studio said that the movie was running too far over budget, which really wasn't George's fault. It would have cost a lot less to film in Israel. I think the bill just for the cars to drive back and forth from the location came to nearly a million dollars. So once the film reached a very high budget they said, '*We've got to get some names into it.*' And the only place was at the end. Everyone was in the last fifteen minutes; me, John Wayne, Sidney Poitier, Pat Boone. I'm sure I've missed others out."

I'm very much alone in this, but I think *The Greatest Story Ever Told* was George Steven's finest achievement and (although at time of writing I haven't yet seen the brand new film *Jesus*) by far the nearest anyone has come to giving us a definitive screen Christ. Also, Max Von Sydow's Jesus remains one of the cinema's most beautiful performances.

Undoubtedly, many will disagree on this. For thousands upon thousands, especially among the Catholics, *Jesus Of Nazareth*, directed by Franco Zeffirelli, is Number One.

(*Above*) *A fabulous "glass-shot" of Rome during Arrius's victory parade.* (Ben-Hur — MGM)

(*Left*) *Charlton Heston in his charioteer's outfit.* (Ben-Hur — MGM)

*The chariots skid precariously around the
turn of the spina.* (Ben-Hur — *MGM*)

Having saved the life of Arrius (Jack Hawkins), Ben-Hur (Charlton Heston) wins freedom from the galleys. (Ben-Hur — MGM)

Messala (Stephen Boyd) takes a quick lead. (Ben-Hur — MGM)

(Above) The mighty hand of God holds back the Red Sea. (Left) While Rameses remains unconvinced of Moses' powers, the prophet commands hail to fall from a clear sky. (The Ten Commandments — Paramount)

(Opposite) Moses (Charlton Heston) warns the people "You are not worthy to receive God's ten commandments." (The Ten Commandments — Paramount)

Moses kills Baka (Vincent Price), the wicked overseer. (The Ten Commandments—Paramount)

Moses, his family and friends, remain in safety while death passes through Egypt. (The Ten Commandments—Paramount)

Dathan (*Edward G. Robinson*) refuses to allow Joshua (*John Derek*) to take Lilia (*Debora Paget*) to safety. (The Ten Commandments—*Paramount*)

"His eye was not dim, nor his natural force abated". (The Ten Commandments—*Paramount*)

Jesus (Max Von Sydow) stands trial. That's John Wayne on the left as the centurion. (The Greatest Story Ever Told – United Artists)

Lot (Stewart Granger) is arrested for murdering the Sodomite prince (Stanley Baker). (Sodom and Gomorrah)

"My God, they're trying to change the Bible."

Robert Powell in his popular portrayal of the Saviour. (Jesus of Nazareth — ITC-RAI)

Lord Lew Grade first conceived of a new film on the life of Christ when he was backing *Moses – The Lawgiver*. Anthony Burgess provided a script which, while presenting the most complete version of Jesus' life so far, was *too* clever, and distorted simple and direct scriptural passages into hard-to-recognise lines of dialogue: ie, Instead of Jesus making clear his point that He was "the resurrection and the life" before raising Lazarus from the dead, He added it almost as an after-thought after bringing Lazarus to life again. This, I suppose, is poetic licence but compared to George Stevens' version, in which the "I am the resurrection" bit is given clear, concise coverage *before* the miracle, Zeffirelli's lost impact.

However, that said, *Jesus Of Nazareth* is, despite its conception as a marathon TV film, cinematically superb, brilliantly directed, overwhelmingly acted by everyone concerned and beautifully scored by Maurice Jarre.

Pre-production began in June, 1974, when Zeffirelli began his search for suitable locations. He decided to concentrate the filming in Tunisia and Morocco.

A cast of international names played the men and women whose lives became involved with the most influential man who ever lived. Among them were Olivia Hussey as Mary, Laurence Olivier as Nicodemus, James Mason as Joseph of Aramathea, Peter Ustinov as Herod, Ernest Borgnine as The Centurian, Anthony Quinn as Caiaphas, Ralph Richardson as Simeon, Rod Steiger as Pilate, Ian McShane as Judas, Ian Holm as Zerah, Anne Bancroft as Mary Magdalene (who, incidently was *not* a prostitute as every film director seems to think she was), Donald Pleasence as Melchior, Christopher Plummer as Herod Antipas, and many, many more who are far too numerous to find the space to mention here.

And, of course, there was Robert Powell as Jesus. I met Robert a couple of years after he'd played this important role and even then the shadow of the part was still clearly over him so that a sense of wonder still seemed to come to him when speaking of the film.

I asked him how a mere mortal tries to portray the Son of God?

"All you can hope to do is get away with it," he told me. "You cannot get close to the part and very rarely can you relate it to your own experience, because there is nothing to get hold of that is within one's own understanding. For my own benefit I had to humanise the motivations and objectives so that *I* had something with which to work because I can't work in a complete vacuum. In some cases I had to invent them because there was nothing else there. Then I had to play them in such a way that they could be construed as something else as well, but I had to have something for myself which was very private. I had to *feel* a little. That was simpler, I must admit, towards the end of the picture. There

were more things to grasp like during the Last Supper. Rather than play a sort of flat mystical approach to the Holy Communion, my own personal approach was that this was the last time I would see my twelve closest friends. It benefited very much from that because it sort of had an over-current of genuine emotion, while almost secondary, although of course it wasn't in the story, and the rest took care of itself. If I'd done it the other way round it would have meant nothing other than a lot of words.

"I don't necessarily think I have different views now than I did when I was doing it, because to be honest I didn't have many views when I was

57

doing it. They varied from day to day. I literally started out thinking one thing and five months later I was changeable. So was Franco. We reshot a lot of stuff that we did at the beginning as the film grew; stuff that I'd played cold, so to speak, and as the months wore on, as we became more involved, we realised that we had made mistakes because it really was trial and error from my point of view.

"You cannot walk onto a film set and just play Jesus. You have to find a way to do it. In many ways, I'm not sure how accurate the analogy is, but it seemed to me that if I'd supplied Jesus with any of my own idiosyncrasies or mannerisms, or tried to give a *performance*, then for every critic who admired the acting there would be twenty people who would say; that is not my Christ. So logically the best thing was to allow the viewer to do a lot of the work; for me to supply more or less a blank canvas, an energy, a presence and let everybody put onto

it their own view, which worked. I think more than any other Biblical epic to date, the response from the people, and we're talking about millions, was unbelievable. We had millions of letters and they all said the same thing; *'That is exactly how I imagined Jesus to be.'* "

If it all sounds like it was very serious and gloomy throughout the seven

months of production, well in many ways it was. But there were also the light hearted moments. During the filming of the Last Supper Bob Powell turned to Ian McShane and said, "What you must do, do quickly."

Ian rose and went to the door. He turned back and, while the cameras were running, said with a dead-pan expression, "So that's two cod, three

(*Right*) *The Nativity scene from the silent production* From The Manger To The Cross. (*Below*) *Franco Zeffireli's unorthodox version of the Crucifixion.* (Jesus of Nazareth — *ITC-RAI*)

skate and twelve chips."

When Peter Ustinov as Herod learnt that a new king had been born he had to scream with rage, ordering all the male children in Bethlehem to be killed. In the middle of his line a rope accidently fell from the rafters over the set and landed directly in front of his face. Ustinov immediately turned and stared into the camera.

"I suppose this is for *me*?" he said wryly.

Ian McShane confirmed for me that making the film was a lot of fun, but that was only natural considering so many people had to work with each other for a seven month period. I also found out that McShane has a sneaking admiration for Judas Iscariot and he gave me a fascinating theory (none of which is given scriptural evidence) on Judas' behaviour.

"I wanted only to play Judas. They first offered me Joseph. I was in California and really bust, and I needed a job. But I turned down Joseph and said I wanted to play Judas. A week later they came back and offered me Judas.

"I wanted to play him as I think he was, which was the original public agent. Judas was the only one who could read among the disciples, the only educated one. They didn't like him a lot, he was a bit too bright for the rest. And when Zeffirelli and I talked about him he came out that way, because Judas was separate from the rest. The mistake he made was in trying to make Jesus into something else, into a political figure. But Judas didn't do it for himself. The money meant nothing to him. When Judas went upstairs he sat on Jesus' *right* hand. He was the *true* believer. He believed too much. It was Peter that turned Him down, that denied Him. Judas never denied Him. Judas said, '*Yes, He is*,' and suffered for it. He believed *too* strongly and thought Jesus wanted to change the the face of the world. But Jesus had a faith and an extraordinary personality, and I think Bob Powell gave the most extraordinary performance.

"They're funny jobs, those. You spend seven months on a film and you're going to become very close to the people in very special ways. They had to take the camera away from Franco because he didn't ever want to finish making the film.

"He's so remarkable a director. I arrived there on Sunday and he said, '*You begin working on Wednesday*.' On Wednesday I get a 3 a.m. call. We did five hours of me scrambling and running and hanging myself. Which was Zeffirelli's way of saying, 'this is how Ill get you into the mood and if I never use it, it doesn't matter.' And he *didn't* use it. But from that day I was secure."

Another actor who remembers his first day on the set is Simon Mac-Corkindale who played a Roman soldier who was the sort of spokesman of the legionaires. He told me, "The very first thing Franco did was have 40 fits when he saw me. The wardrobe department had given me any old costume that

(Left) This time Jesus had Tunisians waving palms and cheering "Hosanna". (Bottom left) Roman Soldiers hail the King of the Jews. (Below) Ian McShane as Judas. (Jesus of Nazareth — ITC-RAI)

didn't fit properly and he went bananas. Before I knew what was happening I had ten people around me all screaming in Italian and I was being pushed and pulled everywhere as they tried to get my uniform to fit. Bits were sent for and bits were taken away until it was right."

I asked Simon, who was involved in a lot of the crowd scenes, how Zeffirelli managed to get the extras to respond to his demands, especially since most of them were Tunisians.

"He had a lot of crowd directors and he was very dilligent in getting the crowd to react in certain ways. Sometimes he went about it in very strange ways, actually saying terrible things to them to get them to respond angrily if that was needed. Sometimes the crowd acted for real because they didn't always understand what was going on, so in fight sequences us Roman soldiers were really finding it hard to remain on our feet as we were jostled by the crowd."

Like the time Stacy Keach as Barabbas was arrested by the Romans. Before the sequence was filmed Zeffirelli ex-plained to the extras in French that they should try and rescue Barabbas, but they would lose. When they began filming the mob went wild. They tore Stacy Keach loose from the bewildered Roman guard, knocking them to the ground, Simon MacCorkindale amongst them.

"My breast plate was absolutely bent and buckled and I had all cuts down my leg as I and some others were trampled under foot," he told me.

The mob began to run away carrying Keach with them.

"No! No!" shrieked Zeffirelli. "My God, they're trying to change the Bible. He's *supposed* to be arrested. Let the soldiers have him."

Whistles were blown and someone turned on a police siren to catch the crowd's attention, but still the mob marched onwards carrying a by now very unhappy and protesting Barabbas.

Finally, when peace was restored, Zeffirelli told the crowd, "I greatly admire your zeal, but could you please let the Romans have Barabbas the next time."

On the next take the Romans finally won Barabbas, but only after a severe tug of war with Keach in the middle.

The filming also had its more dramatic moments, particularly when Robert Powell went through the agonising feat of hanging from the cross. Having been roped to the wooden crosspiece he was hauled up 20 feet to the top of the frame (no conventional cross was used but a large frame to which the crosspieces of all three condemned men were nailed) five times.

During one of the attempts to get Powell's crosspiece in place the wooden beam, with Powell on it, began to swing out of control and the agonised actor called out in a panic.

When he was finally brought down from the cross his wife Babs rushed to the side of her semi-conscious husband. At least now he could begin to appreciate the agony Christ must have gone through in the Garden of Gethsemane.

The scene on film is one of the most harrowing of all the filmed Golgotha sequences. It would have been complete if only Zeffirelli would have had his Centurian, Ernest Borgnine, utter, "Truly this was the Son of God."

Spreading the word in Cinemascope

Dozens of movies about people who somehow become involved in the life and/or death of Christ have sprung up; some of them awful like *Salome*, others competent like *The Robe* and very few brilliant like *Ben-Hur*.

Salome had Rita Hayworth (an early silent production was made starring Theda Bara) dancing the Dance of the Seven Veils in an attempt to *rescue* John the Baptist! I guess the Bible had it all wrong! And then there was Paul Newman (sorry to bring this up, Paul) in *The Silver Chalice* as a young silversmith who disguises the original chalice used by Christ with an outer covering. It was *worse* than *Salome!* At least *Salome* had Stewart Granger who's worth watching in anything.

In 1953 Twentieth Century Fox re-

(*Top right*) *Theda Bara gets a head in* Salome. (*Right*) *Rita Hayworth as* Salome. (*Columbia*)

(*Opposite*) *"They're going to a better kingdom," screams Caligula (Jay Robinson) as Marcellus (Richard Burton) and Diana (Jean Simmons) make their final exit in* The Robe.
(*Below*) *Marcellus stands at the foot of Jesus' cross during the storm.* (The Robe — 20th Century Fox)

leased the vastly entertaining film version of Lloyd C. Douglas book *The Robe*. I won't insult your intelligence by pretending you don't already know this was the first film to be released in Cinemascope.

Richard Burton played the Centurion who supervises Christ's crucifixion and later becomes a convert after seeking out the robe Jesus wore. Victor Mature was the slave Demetrius who escapes to become one of the first Christians, and lovely Jean Simmons was Burton's loved one back home in Rome.

The film had already started in the old almost square ratio before Fox decided to photograph it in Cinema-Scope, a system which threw the director Henry Koster into an enthusiastic revolutionary mood. He worked

out a new technique of directing especially for the letter-box shaped screen. He believed that cutting from one subject to another was no longer necessary. He filmed it so that the actors were suitably positioned round the set so that all could be seen at the same time.

This idea of Koster's was of course preposterous. Another pioneer film in the wide-screen syndrome was Michael Todd's production *Around The World In Eighty Days*, which was the second film to be shot in the producer's own 70 mm process, Todd-AO.

The director, Michael Anderson, told me, "I was told that you should film in one long continuous 'take' because the picture area was so large. But I ignored it and shot as I would have shot any

(*Above*) *Love in Cinemascope in* The Robe – (*20th Century Fox*). (*Above right*) *Burton, Simmons and director Henry Koster relax in between scenes of* The Robe.

(*Right*) *Shirley MacLaine, David Niven and Cantinflas went* Around The World in 80 Days *and Todd-AO*

normal film, and really that changed the thinking because they found that you could cut very effectively with it.

"There were actually two versions; one in Todd-AO and the other in Cinemascope for showing in theatres not equipped with Todd-AO projection. That was Todd's idea. I shot with the two cameras side by side and when I couldn't do it that way I shot the scene first in Todd-AO and then in Cinemascope, and in many cases the chosen 'take' in the Todd-AO version was not necessarily the chosen 'take' in the Cinemascope version. So there are in fact different performances throughout each film. The differences are perhaps infinitely small because it was the same dialogue, the same action, but the performances might be slightly different."

During a brief meeting with Jean Simmons in 1978, she told me of the problems that beset the actors in *The Robe* because of this new process.

"We had no idea at first how difficult it was going to be filming in Cinema-Scope. They had to use more lights, and it got so *hot!* I've never known heat like that in any scene of any other film. We would have to stand there for hours just so they could focus on all of us because we practically had to play scenes standing in a line."

For an epic, there was surprisingly little action in *The Robe*. The most exciting scene was the hand to hand duel Burton has with Jeff Morrow. Of that scene Burton says; "The big fight scene certainly was different. We had to hack our way through that in deadly earnest from beginning to end (due to Koster's reluctance to cut from one shot to another) without a break and no spoofing.

"I suffered not a split skull – as it happened – but split skin on my skull, and a gashed hand."

Fox suffered nothing more than a terrific profit at the box-office and a sequel was immediately called for. It was *Demetrius And The Gladiators* (which, had it been made today, would undoubtedly have been called *The Robe 2*). This was, in fact, the first film to be written specifically with the Cinema-Scope screen in mind.

Victor Mature was again Demetrius, now fighting for his survival in the arena, and Susan Haywood as his

Director Richard Fleischer, Jack Palance and extras in the preserved Roman arena at Verona where much of Barabbas was filmed. (Below left) Barabbas (Anthony Quinn) listens to Jesus' trial from his cell. (Barabbas – Columbia).

(Below right) The film was called Demetrius And The Gladiators but here Demetrius (Victor Mature) preferred the company of Messalina (Susan Hayward) – 20th Century Fox.

yet today strangely underrated.

Producer Dino De Laurentiis conceived the idea of filming Par Lagerkvist's Nobel Prize winning book "Barabbas" when he was making *La Strada*, starring Quinn and directed by Federico Fellini. It was actually Fellini who suggested *Barabbas* as a vehicle for Quinn.

Laurentiis read the book, was "fascinated by the problem of transforming this admittedly difficult work into a motion picture without losing any

Roman "Delilah". Jay Robinson repeated his role (from *The Robe*) of Caligula, a delightfully animated performance that makes the whole thing worth watching. Actually, it wasn't a bad picture and its scenes of gladiators in combat certainly out-spectacled anything its predecessor did.

There was another sort of sequel to *The Robe*, or to be more precise prequel. This was *The Big Fisherman* based on another Lloyd C. Douglas book. Howard Keel starred as the disciple Peter in this wildly inventive story which has

a daughter of Herod Antipas played by Susan Kohner (the daughter that is; Herbert Lom played Herod) falling for an Arabian Prince (John Saxon).

But we are really concerned with the "greats", and without doubt one such picture is *Barabbas*, directed in 1961 by Richard Fleischer. It is in many ways a beautiful film and correctly described as an "intimate spectacle." In the role of Barabbas, the brigand who was freed while Jesus died, Anthony Quinn excelled, giving one of his most masterful performances,

of the literary value and profound religious spirit", and he bought the rights.

At that time Quinn was appearing in the Broadway success "Becket" with Laurence Olivier and the play was obviously in for a marathon run. Laurentiis had to aquire his star with a considerable sum of money.

His next problem was in finding a writer capable of transferring what was undeniably an almost contemporary-styled piece of historical literature, to the screen without harming the flow. Certainly no ordinary Hollywood script-writer could manage it. The task fell to playwright Christopher Fry who had already proven himself adept at providing lyrical speech for *Ben-Hur*.

American director Richard Fleischer met with Fry and Laurentiis and discovered that "we were in agreement about the kind of film we would try to make. I felt that *Barabbas* offered an opportunity to make a rare kind of film best described in such contradictory terms as an 'intimate spectacle'. Against the vividly coloured background of Roman pomp and the awesome pageant of the Crucifixion, we were undertaking a dramatic analysis of one of the most enigmatic complex characters in literature."

The first scene shot, on February 15th 1961, was the Crucifixion at Roccastrado, 120 miles north of Rome. The scene couldn't be repeated on any later day. For this was the only time in a life-span when a total eclipse would occur and Fleischer wanted to capture it on film as part of the death of Christ. It would be the only Crucifixion scene shot without the use of special effects. Nature would provide its own.

Hundreds of local villagers came to watch the scene, and were so overwhelmed at the sight of three lonely crosses on a hill as the sun went out that they dropped to their knees and prayed. This one scene typified the beauty of the whole film and perfectly set the tone for a remarkable, and certainly one of the most innovative, epics of all time.

Another natural setting in the film was the authentic Roman arena that stands in Verona. It has been superbly preserved and little work had to be done by Art Director Mario Chiari on

(*Right*) The body of Jesus is taken down from the cross. (*Below left*) Quinn found a friend during a break in filming. (*Below right*) Barabbas wakes up on his second morning of freedom next to Sara (Katy Jurado). (Barabbas – Columbia)

 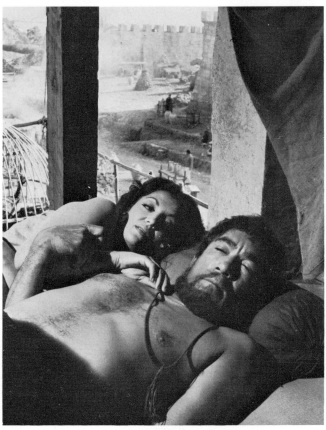

haunting and moving of all the epics, and is a film flawed only by some severe cutting which I feel sure was neither Fleischer's nor film editor's Raymond Poulton's doing. In fact, during the film's premiere in London Dino De Laurentiis erupted with anger when he saw what was on the screen and left the theatre in a rage.

One of the highlights of *Barabbas* is the burning of Nero's Rome. But it was a pale flicker compared to the holocaust that engulfed the Eternal City in MGM's 1950 version of *Quo Vadis*.

Quo Vadis has a colourful history and, as a story, was instrumental in turning the epic into a money-making art form. The novel by Henry Sienkiewicz, published in 1895, is probably the most often filmed book of all time. The first movie version was made in 1901 and ran just a mere ten or twenty minutes. There was a copyright on the book but at the time this did not even occur to Sienkiewicz. However, when

(*Above*) *Barabbas defeats Torvald (Jack Palance) in the arena.* (Barabbas – Columbia)

(*Right*) *The Christians break through the blockade as Rome burns.* (Quo Vadis? – MGM)

restoring it to the magnificence it once displayed 2,000 years ago.

In this arena were assembled 300 gladiators and 9,115 extras to play the gloating spectators. These extras at one time became so caught up in the action that when Barabbas killed Jack Palance's evil Torvald, the crowd began to stream out of the arena. Their hero had been victorious and for them the show was over.

This particular battle between Palance, in a chariot, and Quinn, on foot, took four weeks to film. Twice Palance fell from the chariot, once when a wheel collapsed and again when he crashed into the surrounding marble wall. He also suffered severe sores on his hands where the reins wore away his skin. Quinn also had his problems. Several times he had to leap out of the chariot's way in reality.

For the sulphur mines sequences a real mine was used on Mount Etna in Sicily. When the actors appear with bloodshot eyes on the screen they were not wearing make-up.

For the final scene in the mines episode when an earthquake tears the mine apart, special effects men rigged the whole mine to collapse in a way that was spectacular but safe enough to shoot in.

Barabbas remains one of the most

(Above) The slave Lygia (Deborah Kerr) has the undivided attention of Petronius (Leo Genn), Nero (Peter Ustinov) and Marcus (Robert Taylor).
(Right) Nero watches his favourite sport; Christians v lions. Result – Christians nil, lions full! (Quo Vadis – MGM)

large generators were sent to Italy from the MGM Studios in England. Later it became necessary to borrow from the Italian government a generator from the decommissioned battleship, Vittoria Veneto.

The filmed result is a glorious piece of entertainment, full of ludicrous dialogue, sumptuous photography by Robert Surtees, triumphant trumpet fanfares composed by Miklos Rozsa, action, spectacle, romance, the lot. It also had two very special extras. One was the then unknown Sophia Loren who was among hundreds greeting Robert Taylor's entry into Rome, and the other was Elizabeth Taylor who had been unable to co-star in the film as had been originally planned but who still got in on the act by panicking in the fiery streets of burning Rome.

The relationship between the early Christians and the Roman Empire

another version was released in 1910 the author took action and sued the company, Le Film d'Art, and the film was re-titled and unsuccessfully released.

Sienkiewics finally sold the film rights of his book to the Cines Company in Rome. Directed by Enrico Guazzoni in 1912, this new version ran two hours and included lions rented from a circus, gladiators and professional actors. It was truly the first real epic. In 1924 yet another version was made, again in Rome, and this time, it is claimed, a lion had his just deserts when one of the extras unwittingly provided the beast with a meal – himself!

Sam Zimbalist produced the 1950 version, again in Italy, and Mervyn Le Roy directed it. Handsome and ever-so-dashing Robert Taylor starred as Marcus Vinicius, the Roman General who defied Nero for the love of virginal Deborah Kerr. In his role of Nero, Peter Ustinov gained fame in Hollywood plus an Oscar for Best Supporting Actor.

Before filming could commence the giant Cinecitta Studios had to be reconverted back into a film studio having been used not just for making films but also manufacturing war materials and housing German soldiers.

George Emerson, one of Hollywood's foremost animal experts, managed to round up 63 lions, seven fighting bulls from Portugal, two cheetahs from Afri-

ca and 450 horses, including 50 white ones from Denmark. Five of his lions had to be smuggled past Iron Curtain authorities in Vienna where the authorities were reluctant to issue the necessary permits.

As the film was the first Technicolored picture to be made in Italy, the electrical power supply in Rome was inadequate to energise the hundreds of arc lights needed. So five

was finally made compatible in the 1962 Italian production, Constantine The Great, starring Cornel Wilde in the title role of the first Christian Emperor of Rome. It wasn't at all bad as far as being an all-action adventure was concerned. Historically it failed miserably. But it did give some indication of how an ambitious hero came to be the emperor of not only the Roman world, but the Christian world also.

"I much prefer playing emperors. I get much better treatment at the studio commissary."

Vesuvius blows its top and brings about (The Last Days of Pompeii – RKO)

Then what of the original Imperial Rome? The Rome that was untouched by Christianity and worshipped many gods? It has not been totally ignored by film-makers.

In 1912 the Cines Company of Rome quickly followed their *Quo Vadis?* with *The Last Days Of Pompeii* and there was yet another version in 1926. The first sound version was made in 1935, produced by *King Kong* creator Merian C. Cooper and directed by his *Kong* partner Ernest B. Schoedsack. Willis O'Brien, who had put Kong into motion, created a superb Vesuvius complete with volcanic eruption, plus one of the most impressive arena sequences of all time with the use of miniatures.

In 1959 Sergio Leone made the first Technicolored version with everyone's (well, mine at least) favourite muscleman, Steve Reeves, who made quite a nice living out of playing ancient heroes like Hercules and Goliath, but more of that later.

Going back to the silent screen days there was *Cabiria*, which told of a daughter of a noble Roman family who was abducted by Carthaginians during the Punic Wars. Made in 1913 in Italy, it included such highlights as a sea battle and what was probably the first travelling shot over the giant Temple of Baal.

The first really true hero of Roman history, though not to the Romans, was Spartacus, the gladiator who was plucked from slavery to become the most famous fighter of the Roman arena in history. In 72 BC he and his army of gladiators and slaves made servile war on a Rome still ruled by a Republican Senate.

The story of Spartacus was first dramatised on stage in 1831 with American actor Edwin Forrest playing the part in "The Gladiator." During the

nineteen-fifties an Italian film, *Spartacus The Gladiator*, documented the Servile War in a stark manner, filmed in black and white (no doubt due mainly to a lack of money) with some impressive moments, especially as Spartacus' wife makes a night search over the corpse-shrewn battleground for her husband. The film only suffered from appalling dubbing. It was also far more accurate than the Kirk Douglas version in that Spartacus was never crucified. He died on the battlefield with his friends.

However, Douglas' own production of *Spartacus* made in 1960 is still regarded as the most intelligent of all the epics. It certainly had a distinguished

(Opposite top) Spartacus (Kirk Douglas) leads the gladiatorial army in another victory over Roman forces. (Opposite bottom) While a slave, Spartacus receives a flogging for biting a guard. (Below) The slaves toil in the Libyan desert. (Spartacus—Universal Int.)

cast including Douglas himself as the hero of the title, Laurence Olivier, Peter Ustinov, Jean Simmons, Charles Laughton and Tony Curtis.

I could rave about the film for pages, but my publisher hasn't allotted that much space to me, but suffice to say it is easily one of the greatest motion pictures of all time, directed with marked distinction by a then 31-year-old Stanley Kubrick. Sad that today Kubrick disowns the film, claiming that Kirk Douglas did not allow him the freedom to change the screenplay at will.

"The screenplay could have been improved," claims Kubrick, "but it wasn't."

Kubrick's dissatisfaction with Douglas' overall command of the filming (and it was Kirk's own pet project) is a point I was able to put directly to Douglas. He told me;

"Stanley Kubrick was working for one year with Marlon Brando on *One-Eyed Jacks* while I was preparing *Spartacus*. I had worked a long time with Dalton Trumbo (the writer who had been branded a communist and

subsequently black-listed) and we worked very hard getting the ideal cast. (Trumbo wrote a total of seven scripts before Douglas was satisfied).

"We started shooting with Anthony Mann directing, but I didn't think he was right for this picture. Universal, who put up the money, insisted on using him, but after the first week they said, '*Kirk you were right. You gotta get rid of him.*' I had to tell Anthony, who was a very nice guy, that we had to get somebody else. Later I did *The Heroes Of Telemark* for him because I felt I owed him a picture. (Actually, this made Mann free to direct *El Cid*, his finest picture and biggest success.) In the meantime Kubrick got fired by Brando.

"Now, you must understand that before *Spartacus* I'm the one who set up Kubrick's *Paths Of Glory* because he couldn't get the money. I went to United Artists and raised the financing. Yet before we'd started shooting he'd re-written the whole script, and I refused to do it. He said, '*I want to make it a commercial movie,*' so I said, '*Look, I don't know if it's commercial or not, but the first script was beautiful and that's the one we're gonna use.*' So we did. And in my humble opinion *Paths Of Glory* is the best directed film he's ever done.

"Anyway, I showed him the script of *Spartacus*. He said, 'I'd love to do it,' and the next week I brought him over and introduced him to the cast and he started.

"I think he did some brilliant things. Now if Stanley feels he didn't have enough say in it, I must point out he never started the project. Stanley forgets he had re-written *Paths Of Glory* and I made him reject it. We had many discussions with Trumbo about the script, and Stanley was in on everything. But when he came into the picture it had been cast and the script had been done, and he *did* bring about a lot of changes. The first meeting between Spartacus and Varinia in the cell was originally a dialogue scene. But all the dialogue was taken out and it was all done visually, and that was *Kubrick's* concept. It was brilliant and I'm the first to say it. Stanley is a tremendously talented fellow."

Transferring the book by Howard Fast into a satisfactory screenplay proved a headache. It also upset a lot of people in Hollywood because of Kirk's choice of writer in Trumbo. But Kirk displayed his legendary "go to hell" manner which has characterised his whole career as with his rejection of any studio contracts.

"I remember we made a lot of changes in transferring the book to the screen," Kirk told me. "Howard Fast wrote the

(*Above*) Antoninus (*Tony Curtis*) and Spartacus are forced to fight; the victor to be crucified. (*Right*) While Spartacus comes under the shadow of the cross, his wife Varinia (*Jean Simmons*) is wooed by her husband's judge, Crassus (*Laurence Olivier*). (*Spartacus – Universal Int.*)

first screenplay but it wasn't quite satisfactory and I got Dalton Trumbo. At the time he was using the name Sam Jackson, and I announced that Dalton Trumbo was writing the script with me.''

If Kirk's own account of the Kubrick controversy sounds too biased, I was able to get confirmation from Tony Curtis who told me, ''They held a line on Stanley a lot; Kirk, Eddy Lewis (the producer) and Universal. But Stanley in his own inimitable manner was able to say, '*No, I don't like that, I'd like to try this*,' and he'd get it his way. But it wasn't an easy task because he was dealing with Kirk who was running the company (Bryna Productions) and wanted to make sure the picture was made on *his* terms as he had a lot at stake. But Stanley I think gave that film a style it wouldn't have had if somebody else had directed it. He was diligent in his approach and attack."

As to exactly why Anthony Mann was fired Tony could shed no more light. "I never worked with Tony Mann. But I could see Kirk and Universal just didn't like the way the work was coming out. I met Anthony Mann before the film started. They went off on location and when they came back he wasn't around any more."

The production was fraught with injuries and other health problems. Jean Simmons was forced to undergo surgery which kept her out of production for a month, although she was able to return to the set for one week, under a doctor's supervision, to complete her sequence with Laurence Olivier who was scheduled to return from Hollywood (where the production was made) to England.

Tony Curtis split his achilles tendon and was put into plaster up to his hip after surgery; an accident not met with on the set but on Kirk's tennis court. Douglas also was laid up when a virus knocked him for six for ten days, the first time he had been ill during a picture.

There were the lighter moments too, especially from Peter Ustinov, always ready with a quip (and who had, you'll remember already visited ancient Rome as Nero in *Quo Vadis*). He played a mere lanista in this and at one point he moaned, "I much prefer playing emperors. I get better service in the studio commissary."

The massive and final battle was filmed in Spain where 8,000 soldiers

(Left) Politics in the baths between Crassus, Julius Caesar (John Gavin) and Grachus (Charles Laughton). (Bottom left) Helena (Nina Foch) demands Spartacus' death when Draba (Woody Strode) gets the upper hand. (Bottom right) The gladiators make their desperate, and successful, escape. (Spartacus – Universal Int.)

71

(Above) The servile army and Roman legions meet for the decisive battle. (Right) To protect their beloved leader, the surviving gladiators all claim to be Sparticus. (Below) In more peaceful times, Sparticus and Varinia. (Spartacus – Universal Int.)

from the Spanish army portrayed Roman legionaires and gladiators. In the scene where burning logs are rolled over fleeing Romans, four extras received second-degree burns.

Out of the spectacle emerged a picture with first-rate performances and three-dimensional characters. It remains one of Kirk's own favourites. He told me, "I'm very proud of *Spartacus*. It's difficult to make a big epic picture in which the characters stand out, and I think the actors dominated the film. Stanley Kubrick directed it brilliantly."

The film was particularly interesting in its depiction of a very young Julius Caesar, played by John Gavin, before his days as a great Roman general. When it came to making films about the famous assassination, producers generally turned to Shakespeare's drama. As early as 1908 Vitagraph produced a number of one-reel Shakespearean movies, including *Julius Caesar*. There was another version in 1914 but the most famous, and probably the best Shakespearean film of all, was MGM's 1952 production, directed by Joseph L. Mankiewicz.

Mankiewicz always maintained that the film should have been called *Brutus*, since he, as played by James Mason, dominated the tragedy. Caesar himself, played by Louis Calhern, is bumped off half way through the story. For me the hero is Mark Antony, superbly portrayed by Marlon Brando who pip-

ped Paul Scofield at the post for the role.

Actually, it was hardly an epic. Most of the costumes were those used in *Quo Vadis* and the only battle sequence lasted all but a minute. Whether the brief skirmish was due to the minute budget or Mankiewicz's distaste of battle scenes, no-one really knows although the director insists it was the latter.

In the part of Cassius was one of British Theatre's greats, John Gielgud, who turned up wearing Ceasar's robes in the 1969 production of *Julius Caesar*. Charlton Heston headed the cast as Antony. There was also Richard Johnson, superb as Cassius, and Jason Robards, totally miscast as Brutus. Richard Chamberlain was fine as Octavius and Robert Vaughan was brilliant as Casca. Poorly directed by Stuart Burge, it was nevertheless a colourful, at times exciting and compellingly acted (overall) picture. Produced by Peter Snell, it was the forerunner to the unfairly criticised and a one-day-to-be-discovered classic, *Antony And Cleopatra*, starring Heston as Antony and directed by him also. That film's biggest flaw, and one of its few, was the choice of Hildegard Neil as Cleopatra. Miss Neil is a superb actress, but not a Cleopatra. That said, John Castle was outstanding as Octavius and Eric Porter stole the film with his scene in which he described "the barge she sat in."

It is difficult to explore one picture without the other, especially in talking to Peter Snell about them. What follows is an interview with Snell which I conducted in his Pinewood Studios office.

M.M. Shakespeare on film is a gamble and you gambled twice.

P.S. A gamble that in most cases has been lost. I took a gamble and lost twice, no doubt about that. Nobody got badly hurt because we made them for such a good price because they were both a labour of love. They cost a million and a half dollars and nobody made a great deal of money either.

M.M. You talk about how little you spent on the films, but they both looked expensive.

P.S. That's true. That's where I got my early training in getting

(Top) *Julius Caesar (Louis Calhern) makes his triumphant entry into Rome.* (Middle) *Antony (Marlon Brando) comforts Caesar; "Fear him not, Caesar. He is not dangerous."* (Bottom) *The none-event of the film; the briefest battle in cinema history.* (Julius Caesar—MGM)

(*Above*) *Producer Peter Snell on location for* Julius Caesar *in Spain with Chamberlain who played Octavius.* (*Top left*) *Brutus (Jason Robards) discovers the body of his friend Cassius (Richard Johnson).* (*Right*) *Cassius' troops stand ready for action.* (Julius Caesar — *Commonwealth United*)

production values on the screen. *Antony And Cleopatra* was a case in point. We simply structured it very carefully with stock footage from *Cleopatra* and *Ben-Hur*. We looked at the costumes in those films and designed our costumes to match and then structured very tight action sequences with Heston fighting sixteen people and then cutting to stock footage where we suddenly had thousands of people fighting. We built the pyramids in Spain which in those days was still an inexpensive place to shoot. *Julius Caesar* was a different matter. That was made for Commonwealth United, and for me was personal experience. Take the Shakespeare away and a sheer logistic production exercise was, for me at 28, a tremendous opportunity to throw myself into the kind of films people just weren't making. You just didn't get a chance at that age to produce a picture of that size.

M.M. In both films you had Joe Cannut as 2nd Unit Director.

P.S. ... who's always doubled Chuck Heston and who, God knows, is son of Yak, and he made the battles look good and I learned an immense amount about staging a battle from a production point of view. A fascinating exercise for me in *Antony* was I was producing a picture that was directed by its star. As critic-

ally ill-fated perhaps as it was, 'cos God knows how they crucified it, it was again good experience. They just didn't like it. Hildegard, alright. Jesus Christ, Cleopatra and Hitler have to be three impossible roles. But when Heston decided he wanted to make the film we had to find a Cleopatra and in Heston's book "The Actor's Life" he talks at great length about

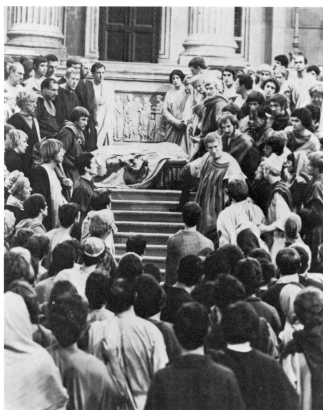

The "Friends, Romans, countrymen" scene from (Top left) Joseph Mankiewicz's version for MGM and (Above right) Stuart Burge's less inspiring, though more spectacular, version. (Left) The killing of Caesar was one of the more effective scenes in Commonwealth United's Julius Caesar

how he arrived at the choice. Everyone said we were wrong to choose Hildegard and today everyone feels that's what cost us the film. Both Heston and I made that film for no salary at all so in a certain sense I paid for that certain education.

M.M. You even managed to get some of the Samuel Bronston costumes (as used in *The Fall Of The Roman Empire*). How did you manage that?

P.S. They were still there. Heston's involvement helped because he had done *El Cid* and *55 Days At Peking*. They had been bought by a lot of costume companies in Madrid so we managed to get a lot of that stuff together and that made it a lot cheaper. I set out to make a very commercial *Julius Caesar*. I was determined to make an entertaining *Julius Caesar* that every critic and every scholar would hate. How else could I cast Robards as Brutus, Chamberlain as Octavius and Robert Vaughan as Casca? And at the end of the day, dammit, they were good. It was a blatantly commercial Shakespeare. In America they run it constantly on television.

M.M. Can you see Heston directing again?

P.S. I don't think he would. He directed *Antony* because we could not find a director that was available. Heston said, '*O God, I know the play so well, I'll have a go with the right cameraman.*' And he did a very creditable job of directing that picture; I think it was one of the more successful attempts of an actor to direct himself because most of them are ego trips that come desperately unstuck. Unlike most guys who have directed themselves and probably haven't succeeded and wanted desperately

to be film directors, Heston never wanted to be a director and he hasn't directed since. But he just found himself in a position where the only way he was going to get that film made was to direct himself.

For Heston, *Antony And Cleopatra* provides him with one of his most powerful performances and despite the critical butchers who slaughtered the movie, it remains one of the better efforts to relate the story of the Queen of Egypt.

The first ever film of *Cleopatra* was made in France in 1906. Another silent attempt was produced in Italy, but the famous one of that era was the 1916 American version with "Vamp" Theda Bara in the title role. There was of course DeMille's early talkie with

(Opposite top left) Charlton Heston displayed his vivid imagination as a Director by staging a gladiatorial combat during the first meeting between Antony (Heston) and Octavius (John Castle) in Antony and Cleopatra. *(Opposite top right) Heston, the Director.*

(Opposite bottom) Antony's forces of Romans and Egyptians face the forces of Octavius.

(Above) Antony puts himself in the very midst of the battle. (Left) Close-up shots such as these were interspliced with stock shots from Ben-Hur *and* Cleopatra *to create the sea battle. (Antony and Cleopatra)*

Claudette Colbert, and in 1945 Rank produced the most ambitious British production up to that time, *Caesar And Cleopatra* with Vivien Leigh and Claude Rains in the title roles. It was at the very beginning of that production that Vivien Leigh told her happy husband, Laurence Olivier, she was pregnant. Six weeks after shooting had begun Vivien had a miscarriage. She allowed herself only a few days convalescence and her troubled mind actually gave a deeper dimension to her portrayal.

While Theda Bara, Claudette Colbert and Vivien Leigh were all to leave their mark in *Cleopatra*'s screen history, not one of them could compete in pure ballyhoo and news-headlines with Elizabeth Taylor in the 1958–59–60–61–62–63 production that almost ruined Twentieth Century Fox. The making of this film, surely the most troubled production ever, would justify a book, and indeed the producer Walter Wanger's diary on the making of this film was published. It has a history not easily telescoped into a few pages, but for those unfamiliar with the bizarre tale, here it is in the briefest possible terms.

ACT ONE: 1958; Walter Wanger and Fox president Spyros Skouras discuss the possibility of filming a two million dollar version of *Cleopatra*. Potential leads include Joan Collins, Suzy Parker and Elizabeth Taylor. 1959; A writer begins work on the script. Laurence Olivier is suggested to play Caesar. In July Liz Taylor is offered the role and she demands a fee of one million dollars plus 10 per cent of the profits, thinking they'll go away. Fox accept! October; Rouben Mamoulian is assigned to direct. Fox production chief Buddy Adler, just before his death, orders the unit to England, and art director John De Cuir (who had begun building the city of Alexandria in Hollywood where they were originally going to film, and then erected Temples in Rome when it was decided to move to Italy) now finds himself building Rome at Pinewood Studios. Are you with me so far? By now the budget has risen to six million! Peter Finch is now playing Caesar and Stephen Boyd is Antony.

(Right) A less loving moment between Antony and Cleopatra, Heston's Cleo played by Hildegard Neil. (Bottom right) Theda Bara's Cleopatra couldn't even afford a decent bra! (Bottom left) Vivien Leigh and Claude Rains in the expensive Caesar and Cleopatra *(Rank).*

Liz Taylor's health suffers in the English climate and just over ten minutes of film is shot. Mamoulian quits.

ACT TWO: 1961; Joseph L. Mankiewicz takes over direction reluctantly but decides to take the money and bear the fifteen week schedule. March; Liz Taylor is rushed to hospital with pneumonia and when she is given one hour to live an emergency tracheotomy is performed. Five days pass and she's out of danger but in need of long recuperation. Fox shuts down production. Skouras orders the production moved back to California for a summer start. John De Cuir again begins construction on Alexandria and Rome. Meanwhile, Mankiewicz has his sights set on filming in Rome. Skouras agrees and De Cuir is left with three months to build everything again in Rome.

ACT THREE: Mankiewicz, unhappy with all previous script efforts, begins work on his own screenplay of *Cleopatra*. (Throughout production he spends his nights at the type-writer and his days behind a camera.) His fifteen weeks become eight months and still nothing filmed. Finch and Boyd have both quit. Rex Harrison takes over as Caesar and Richard Burton as Antony. In September, 1961, Eddie Fisher and

(*Left*) *Art Director John De Cuir wondering where* Cleopatra *will take him next.*
(*Below*) *John De Cuir's beautiful set for* Cleopatra *which he built in England at Pinewood Studios.*

wife Liz Taylor arrive in Rome. 25th September; the first scene is actually shot by Mankiewicz. Burton spends first three months in Rome twiddling his thumbs . . . . . finally doing first scene with Taylor in January, 1962. The same month, rumours of a romance between Taylor and Burton blossom and Eddie Fisher wilts. By the end of 1961 some twenty million dollars has been poured into *Cleopatra*. By July Mankiewicz is mentally and physically exhausted and rejoices when he shoots the final scenes in Egypt. Then, suddenly, Darryl F. Zanuck takes over the presidency of Fox and *Cleopatra*.

ACT FOUR: In October Zanuck views the first rough cut which Joe has edited in two months. Zanuck takes the film out of Joe's hands and puts it in the palms of his right-hand man Elmo Williams to edit. Mankiewicz is fired. Zanuck and Williams discover they cannot construct a finished print and, in December 1962, Mankiewicz is re-hired to shoot additional footage. In February 1963, Mankiewicz re-shoots opening scene, continues with additional scenes and finishes on March 5, 1963. His fifteen weeks have become two years and the two million dollar budget a staggering forty million. THE END . . . . . almost!

What happened during the film's distribution was madness. The film continued to be cut and re-cut until there were at least three different versions in circulation. All we can do is view what is available, especially the television release print which seems to be the most complete, and get an idea of what could have been the greatest epic of all time.

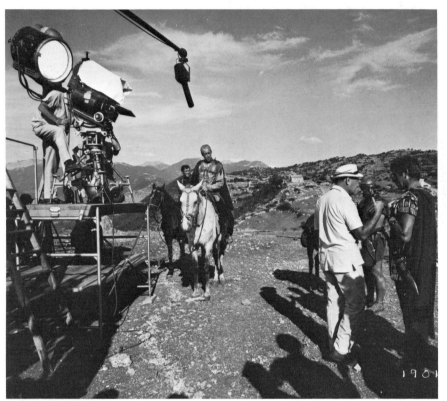

(Right) This version of the opening scene of Cleopatra *was scrapped. When it was re-shot Burton had gone home and so didn't appear. (Below) Shooting the lavish naval battle for* Cleopatra.

(Opposite left) Elizabeth Taylor in her most famous role, Cleopatra. (Opposite top right) The most famous love affair in history between Antony (Richard Burton) and Cleopatra takes fruit. (Opposite bottom right) Cleopatra wins Rome with a wink. (Cleopatra — 20th Century Fox)

It's worth taking a look at some of the more personal experiences that some of the co-stars had making *Cleopatra*, whether they appeared in the final cut(s) or not.

Stephen Boyd long remembered the good times and once recalled, "One day several of us were reading for the part of Antony, and Elizabeth was ill, so we went around to her house just as she was getting up. And God! She's the most beautiful thing. This vision came out of the bedroom.

"Peter Finch was going to play Caesar. He and I spent most of our time in the studio bar. One day we drank just about as much as we could and then in walked this guy. He told us that new costumes were ready for us to try on and that we were wanted in wardrobe for fittings. Finchie and I staggered out of the bar, up to wardrobe and I doubt whether you'll ever see a funnier sight than me and Finchie trying on Roman togas!"

George Cole spoke to me about his months on the film playing a mute aide to Julius Caesar.

(Right) The conspirators (including Doug Wilmer, Kenneth Haigh, Michael Horden and Roddy McDowell) gather on the Senate steps. (Below) Octavius (Roddy McDowell) waylays Antony. (Below Right) Joseph Mankiewicz got a second stab at assassinating Caesar in Cleopatra *(20th Century Fox).*

"What was so depressing was I had no lines to learn in the evenings," he said. "I had to have a fully laid-on beard and I used to have to go to make-up at five o'clock every morning and this beard was painstakingly put on. It was very good, put on by an Italian who was a bit like a chef when the boss does it all and the boys stand around handing him the utensils. I went out there, incidently, for fourteen weeks and stayed eighteen months. And after six months of getting up at five every morning, I said to the make-up man, '*Why do you lay on this beard, why don't you have one already made for me?*' And he said, '*I know when actors talk, they don't like to feel stiff around*

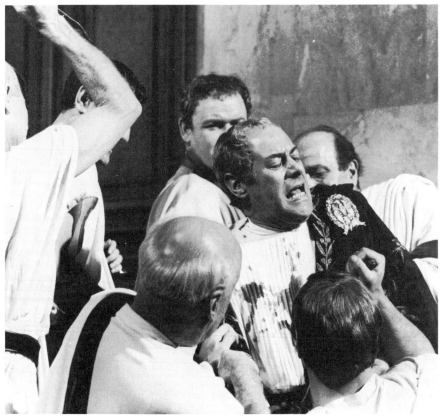

the mouth,' and I said, 'Yes, *but I'm playing a mute*,' and he hadn't taken it in that I was playing this mute, and he continued to lay it on.

"I took a flat in Rome and the money they gave me was just for expenses and it was certainly more than I needed. I got so depressed out there. I grew to hate Michelangelo! It's a very small place, Rome, and everywhere you go *his* work is there."

Richard O'Sullivan was just a mere slip of a lad when he played Cleopatra's scheming brother. He appeared in only one scene yet he too spent many long months waiting in Rome for his glorious moment before the camera.

Said Richard; "I went out for what was supposed to be six weeks, shooting one day a week. It turned into eight months during which I did about eight days work. I stayed in a grand hotel, and every Monday morning a man came and gave me stacks of money. But after two months it got a bit boring, so I asked them if I could get away for the weekend. They said, '*Sure, Richard; go to Naples or Sicily*.' I said, '*Actually*

(*Top left*) *Marcus Aurelius* (*Alec Guinness*), *flanked by Timonides* (*James Mason*) *and Livius* (*Stephen Boyd*), *greets the leaders of his empire.* (*Below*) *Livius and his one-time friend Commodus battle it out in chariots.* (The Fall Of The Roman Empire — Samuel Bronston)

I want to go to London.' So I got on the Friday night flight, saw Chelsea play on Saturday, played charity football on Sunday and arrived back in Italy on Monday. For the next six months I just hung around Lording it!"

What could still prove to be the definitive Roman drama, complete with political intrigues and sexual depravity, is *I Claudius*, if it ever gets filmed. The Alexander Korda version starring Charles Laughton was abandoned in 1937 when the leading lady, Merle Oberon, was injured in a car crash. During the sixties J. Lee Thompson was fully prepared to direct a new attempt, but this never got off the ground. The subject seemed jinxed, a jinx many thought broken when the BBC made the brilliant serial for television. A short time later the producer, Martin Lisenmore, died. John Hurt, who was so superb as Caligula, told me, "It *must* be jinxed."

Until *I, Claudius* reaches our screens I'll be satisfied with what, for me, is the not-quite-but-nearest-to-being-definitive Roman epic; *The Fall Of The Roman Empire*, in 1964.

It was Samuel Bronston's second to last production before he went out

of business, and boasted a superior cast; Sophia Loren as Lucilla, daughter of Marcus Aurelius, played by Alec Guinness. James Mason was Timonides, the gentle Greek philosopher. Christopher Plummer gave what I think is still his best performance as the corrupt Commodus, son of the Emperor Aurelius. Only Stephen Boyd, so visually impressive in a Roman Tribune's uniform, failed to make an impact, but that was more to do with his fictitious and poorly defined character than his already proven acting ability.

Boyd's hero, Livius, was a role Bronston had originally offered to Charlton Heston straight after their collaboration on *El Cid*, directed by Anthony Mann who was again in on this one. Heston could have done wonders with the part, particularly through his perseverence on script improvements. Instead he turned it down, but agreed to do Bronston's inferior *55 Days At Peking*. Bronston, so eager to have this star for a second time, postponed *Roman Empire* and went straight into *Peking*. If only Heston had chosen otherwise!

Today, Sir Alec Guinness can't

remember anything about the film.

"I never even saw it," he told me.

"Well, I enjoyed your performance immensely," I told him.

"Oh, you *can't* have!" he insisted.

I don't know if Sir Alec remembers being offered the role of Marcus Aurelius, but before deciding to take it he went away on a fishing holiday, and then flew to Rome and spent four hours meditating before the statue of Aurelius on the Capitoline Hill.

When Sophia Loren flew from Paris to Madrid to begin her role of Lucilla, the airport almost came to a standstill as she was mobbed by hundreds of screaming fans.

For me the biggest star of the film was the mighty Roman Forum, surely the most impressive and beautiful set ever built. It was constructed on the plains of Las Matas, 16 miles from Bronston's studios in Madrid, designed by Veniero Colesanti and John Moore. Bronston ordered that it be a three-dimensional set so it could be filmed from any angle.

Five months before filming Yakima Canutt rounded up 1,500 horses from Spain and Portugal and put them through a rigorous training course,

teaching them how to fall for the battle scenes.

For the Battle of the Four Armies Bronston recruited 8,000 of General Franco's Spanish army. (They'd previously been employed also on *King Of Kings* and *El Cid*, and a story started to circulate that one day Generalissimo Franco said to his Minister of War, "It has been a long time since I inspected the army. Fix a parade." To which the nervous Minister replied, "Sorry, Generalissimo, it cannot be done. The army is making a movie for Samuel Bronston again.")

About that massive battle sequence, Mann explained, "If you stretch out thousands of soldiers on a flat terrain

(Top right) Alec Guinness warms himself in the cold Sierra Guadarrama mountains. (Below) The other Roman game; backgammon. (Bottom) Timonides gets a warm reception from Ballomar (John Ireland), the barbarian leader. (The Fall Of The Roman Empire—Samuel Bronston)

(Opposite) The coronation of Commodus in the mighty Forum. (The Fall Of The Roman Empire — Samuel Bronston)

those in the rear are so diminished by distance that you lose the effect of their numbers. To avoid this we located a corrugated plain near Manzanares El Real. When the soldiers battled over the undulating plain those in the rear were elevated into better view of the cameras and their numbers seemed endless in the scene."

Actual shooting began on January 14, 1963 in the Sierra Guadarrama mountains for the opening scenes. Anthony Mann wanted snow for this portion of the film. He got the worst winter weather in 50 years with temperatures well below freezing. To warm themselves, the stars practised skating figure 8s on the frozen lakes.

Only Anthony Mann seemed to keep satisfactorily warm. No wonder, since he wore a special cold-weather suit ordered from the London firm which made an electrically-heated jacket for King George VI when he suffered from lung trouble.

James Mason was heard on the set to be warming himself with thoughts of how they were going to kill him off in this film. "I once died in six successive pictures," he said. "In this one they strap a bit of wood to my chest beneath my toga, stretch some piano wire from it and send a javelin hurtling along the wire. Should the wire accidentally go slack it will be a most *realistic* death."

The only death that occurred as a result of the film, a slow death at that,

(*Left*) *Commodus* (*Christopher Plummer*) *duels with Livius.* (*Top left*) *A busy time for Livius; he also has to deal with Sohamus* (*Omar Shariff*). (*Top right*) *Sohamus and his unwilling wife, Lucilla* (*Sophia Loren*). (*Bottom*) *Roman forces clash with barbarians.* (The Fall Of The Roman Empire — *Samuel Bronston*)

was of the Bronston organisation. It lived just long enough to make *The Magnificent Showman* before its demise. Samuel Bronston did have another attempt at producing an epic in the early seventies when he actively prepared *Isabella Of Spain* starring Glenda Jackson.

In an interview with Miss Jackson I asked her why the film never got made.

"Bronston couldn't get the money," she said. "It's as simple as that. It was a big budgeted film, made in an age when that sort of budget was unthinkable. It was like six million pounds. If he'd wanted to have made a disaster movie he probably would have got the money.

"My agent calls him *the pirate king*. Bronston is a wonderful, marvellous man, but the industry has changed too radically for someone as individual and as enormous as him. He was completely independent and he had a large and expensive view of what films were about. He's an expensive personality, but the film industry has been taken over by accountants and they don't like expensive personalities, which is a shame because I find him delightful. A very warm man.

"The film had gone a long way into preparation. The script still wasn't quite right. He had the most incredible facilities from the Spanish government. They were allowing him to shoot in all the actual palaces Isabella had been in, several of which I believe are now monasteries and convents. The incumbents were going to be turned out to facilitate the shooting. I think he'd got the whole of the Spanish army to use as extras. The sets were being built. He'd hired the costume designers. Materials were being especially woven and painted. He'd got his entire crew virtually. It was all there waiting and then he hurtled into a suit about money and just couldn't get it together."

It was a long, long way from the glorious triumph of *El Cid*.

(*Below*) *Dignitaries from every part of the empire gather before the emperor.* (*Right*) *Commodus allows Livius to meet with Lucilla.* (The Fall Of The Roman Empire – Samuel Bronston)

"Sophia Loren probably wasn't aware that I wasn't talking to her because I was supposed to be dead."

Charlton Heston as El Cid, *preparing for the trial by combat.* (Samuel Bronston).

It was in the summer of 1960 when Charlton Heston was offered the role of *El Cid*, Spain's greatest hero who lived in the 12th Century and who secured Spain from the marauding African Moors of Ben Yusof. Heston immediately plunged into research and discovered that the script by Philip Yordon seemed incomplete concerning the Cid's motivations. Chuck, in his search for a deeper insight into the character, met with Yordon and Anthony Mann in Paris and there he learned of Yordon's concept of the Cid; a sort of Job character. Chuck found himself hooked, but this was purely on Yordon's ability to verbally relate a film. Writing it was not so easy. Heston was promised a revised script within the next two and a half weeks. Before leaving for America, Heston was given about thirty pages of the new script to wet his appetite.

Two and a half weeks later the script had not been completed. Chuck was full of misgivings. Still, it was too late. He was committed to the project. He arrived in Spain to begin preparations on the film, and, as yet, no Chimene, El Cid's wife, had been found. Sophia Loren seemed a strong possibility.

On October 13 word came that Sophia had agreed to do the film. Since she had insisted her scenes be shot first it meant rearranging the whole schedule. However, Sophia, like Chuck, had many misgivings about the script and, when Chuck went over to talk to Yordon about the screenplay's progress, he found the writer preparing to leave for Rome to soothe La Loren.

Two days later, while Chuck was practising swinging his broadsword while mounted on the beautiful white horse representing Babieca, a muddled message came through about whether Sophia was still in the film or out. A day later the muddle was sorted out. Loren was out. Jeanne Moreau was named the most likely candidate for Chimene. Another day passed and Sophia was in again.

Before any cameras turned Tony Mann met with Heston to assure him that the forthcoming script changes would improve matters no end. These revisions turned out later to be Sophia's. They worked, too.

Sophia's arrival in Madrid (as it would later be for *Roman Empire*) was a humdinger. Chuck Heston saved her from being engulfed by the mob by hurrying her into the waiting car, and found he liked her after all the fuss. The next day (November 14) filming finally began.

Christmas came and went, filming continued, and it got very, *very* cold. Sophia suffered more than Heston. She would stand, embraced by Chuck, her teeth clacking together like castanets. Chuck finally convinced Mann to finish the dialogue inside the studio. It was about this time that Ben Barzman

The zealots are defeated by the Romans.
(King of Kings — *MGM*)

The Sermon on the Mount. (King of Kings —
MGM).

(Above) Spartacus (Kirk Douglas) and his wife Varinia (Jean Simmons). (Opposite top). Spartacus (Kirk Douglas) leads his servile army. (Opposite bottom) Draba (Woody Strode) overpowers Spartacus. (Spartacus – Universal Int.)

(Right) Samson (Victor Mature) and Delilah (Hedy Lamarr) (Samson and Delilah – Paramount)

(*Above*) Julius Caesar (Rex Harrison) has Cleopatra (Elizabeth Taylor) crowned Queen of Egypt. (*Right*) Caesar and Cleopatra. (Cleopatra – 20th Century Fox).

(*Opposite top left*) Mark Antony (Richard Burton) in battle. (*Opposite top right*) "Et tu Brute". (*Opposite bottom*) The mighty Roman Forum. (Cleopatra – 20th Century Fox)

Octavius (Richard Chamberlain) and Mark Antony (Charlton Heston) before battle. (Julius Caesar – Commonwealth United).

(Opposite) Charlton Heston as Mark Antony (Below) Antony addresses the crowd over Caesar's body. (Julius Caesar – Commonwealth United)

Livius (Stephen Boyd) lashes out against the corrupt regime of Commodus (Christopher Plummer). (The Fall Of The Roman Empire — *Samuel Bronston*)

Commodus descends into the Forum and the barbarians await their fiery end. This tremendous set for Samuel Bronston's The Fall Of The Roman Empire *was built in Spain and was three dimensional, as was Bronston's Peking in* 55 Days At Peking.

The Battle of the Five Armies. (The Fall Of The Roman Empire — *Samuel Bronston*)

was brought in to improve the script.

As time wore on Sophia began to play up. They all worked hard throughout one whole day on the scene where El Cid, now older and bearded, tells an ever-youthful Chimene (Sophia wouldn't allow the make-up man to age her) of his disappointments. Just as they seemed to get it right Sophia packed up and went home.

When it came for Chuck to die with an arrow protruding from his chest while lying in bed, Sophia turned up late *again*. He was so damned mad he refused to talk to her. "She probably wasn't aware that I wasn't talking to her," he told me, "because I was supposed to be dead."

Two days later Sophia finished the last of her scenes. Then four hours later, she fell down the stairs and broke her shoulder. Before she left for Rome Heston turned up with flowers and made amends for their differences in professional standards.

Things didn't always go smooth even after that. But it never does when making epics. Anthony Mann had a run-in with Yak Cannut over who should play with the three thousand extras in the big battle scenes. Yak wanted to be left to do his job at directing the battles. Mann wanted to do it himself. When they got around to filming the breathtaking trial by combat, Yak said, "Let me shoot it, or I'm through." Mann finally gave in, and the results on screen couldn't be better. The trial by combat stands alongside *Ben-Hur*'s chariot race as one of the most exciting sequences ever filmed.

Samuel Bronston was over the moon

(*Above left*) *Everything stops for tea for Heston and John Fraser.* (*Above*) *The Cid re-united with his wife Chimene (Sophia Loren).* (*Bottom*) *The Cid dies in the presence of his wife and his king (John Fraser).* (*El Cid – Samuel Bronston*).

with Heston for his contribution to the film, and well he might be. While Anthony Mann did some brilliant things with the camera (notably in the final sequence when the dead Cid, strapped to his horse, rides out to meet the Moors to the awesome organ chords of Miklos Rozsa), the polish of the film also had much to do with Heston's perseverence at getting so much changed from the start. Whoever was to be thanked, Bronston couldn't thank Heston enough and promptly bought him a Jaguar XKE.

Heston was disappointed with the finished result. He thinks it is a fine film, but not a great one. "It should have been the greatest epic ever," he told

Trial By Combat In El Cid

(*From left to right*) *The opponents Rodrigo—the Cid and Don Martin (Christopher Rhodes) clash. The Cid is knocked from his steed. Rodrigo brings Don Martin down. Don Martin has the upper-hand. With the larger sword, Rodrigo begins to hold his own. Having lost much blood himself, Rodrigo finally conquers his foe.*

with Gary Raymond, John Fraser and Douglas Wilmer from Britain, Geraldine Page from France, Herbert Lom from Czechoslovakia, Raf Vallone from Italy, Missimo Serato from Spain and, of course, Heston from America and Loren from Italy.

No doubt Heston's epic appeal had much to do with the film's enormous success in 1961. It was in that same year that Bronston offered him *The Fall Of The Roman Empire*. The research-conscious Heston again threw himself into the material of that period and decided the script had little in common with what actually happened. For nearly four months he thought about doing the film, and towards the end of 1961 he finally turned Bronston down. No sooner had he freed himself from *Roman Empire* than Bronston, determined to have Heston in his next film, ensnared him for *55 Days At Peking*, shelving the *Roman* project for another year.

It was Nicholas Ray, who would direct *Peking*, who approached Chuck

(*Top*) *The Cid enters Valencia.* (*Above*) *Offered the crown, the Cid refuses it* (*Above left*) *The night before battle.* (*Right*) *In the morning the Cid leads his troops out to meet the Moors.* (El Cid – Samuel Bronston)

me. "If William Wyler had made *El Cid*, it *would* have been the greatest epic ever." Well, for me *El Cid* is a great film, with Heston giving one of his strongest performances ("I think in the first half I was not too good. I was better in the second half"), and Miklos Rozsa's score is probably the best he's ever done, and that includes *Ben-Hur*.

The rest of the cast fared well also. It was certainly internationaly cast with a story outline set in the Boxer Rebellion. Heston thought it might prove an interesting period to explore and also liked the idea of working for Ray.

After three meetings with Ray and Philip Yordon, who was working on yet another unfinished script, Chuck gave in and said "yes." It wasn't the best decision he ever made. He definitely felt uneasy about the whole thing, but he had confidence in Nick Ray.

Meanwhile, while Peking was being constructed in Spain out of what

(*Right*) *The Cid is wounded in battle.* (*Below*) *Fanez (Massimo Serato) comes to the Cid's aid.* (*Below right*) *The Cid receives his dying wish from his king.* (*Bottom left*) *As the dead Cid rides into legend, he is watched by his wife and twin daughters.* (*Bottom right*) *On the set of El Cid; producer Bronston and star Heston.* (*El Cid — Samuel Bronston*)

started out as the Roman Forum for *Empire*, Heston went to Hawaii to make *Diamond Head* for director Guy Green with whom Chuck established a very satisfactory working relationship. During the spring of 1962, Nick Ray phoned Chuck in Hawaii and announced that they were seeking Ava Gardner to play the Russian Countess, a piece of casting that, in Heston's estimation, and correctly it proved, was a *miss*. Ava Gardner was just *too* American.

A couple of days later Heston finished on *Diamond Head*, and immediately there began frantic transatlantic phone calls, one from Ray in London, another from Bronston in Spain, both trying to bring Chuck around to their way of thinking regarding Ava. Chuck began

(*Right*) *The not-so-happy stars of* 55 Days At Peking; *Charlton Heston, Ava Gardner and David Niven.* (*Below*) *The giant set of Peking built in Spain.* (Samuel Bronston)

(Top Left) Sir Arthur Robertson (David Niven) and Major Lewis (Charlton Heston) appear before the Chinese Empress. (Top right) Sir Arthur's son is wounded as the uprising begins. (Above) Lewis tells Teresa (Lynne Sue Moon) that her father has been killed by the Boxers. (Above right) Lewis meets with Natalia (Ava Gardner) at the hospital where she works as a nurse. (55 Days At Peking – Samuel Bronston)

to wish he was not even in the film.

Arriving in Madrid towards the end of May, Heston lunched with Ray and Bronston and tried to solve the problem over the casting of the leading lady. How about Deborah Kerr? She won't do it. Mercouri or Jeanne Moreau? Hmmmm! Bronston made it clear that all the European distributors wanted Ava Gardner and Bronston needed the support of the distributors.

Another meeting with all the Bronston brass, and Heston won a pleasing round with everyone agreeing to ignore the distributors and get a major European star. A few days later David Niven confirms he is in and Mercouri demands major re-writes if she is to be in.

A month later and it's Ava Gardner back in. At a late night script session with Nicholas Ray, Ava went into a complete attack on her part and Chuck Heston, who had proved his heroism when he rescued Sophia Loren from hundreds of screaming fans, withdrew. Nick Ray wasn't Sophia Loren and could look after himself!

On the first day's shooting Ava showed more than just first day nerves. Nick's handling of her was very delicate. As filming progressed the script didn't. Heston and Niven began making up their own lines and once again Ben Barzman had to be recruited to try and improve the screenplay.

Ava was starting to turn up late on the set and one day she stormed out when she complained that a Chinese extra had been photographing her. She took a three hour long lunch break and returned . . . . . and promptly walked off again. Such conduct resulted in much of Ava's scenes being cut down, and for one scene Nick Ray gave all her lines to Paul Lucas, who was playing Dr. Steinfeldt. This infuriated her even more.

On September 11, Nicholas Ray was preparing the day's first set-up when he suddenly collapsed with a heart attack. He was bundled into a car and driven straight to hospital. When Ava finally arrived on the set Chuck told her of the tragedy. As if admitting her guilt, Ava worked well the rest of the morning under the direction of Andrew Marton, whose job was really in handling the action.

When it was apparent that Ray could not return to work (in fact he never directed again) Heston convinced Bronston to hire Guy Green to finish the film. There were only two major scenes to be done, but when Guy arrived he decided that all of Ava's

(*Right*) *Chrysagon* (*Charlton Heston*),
accompanied by Boros (*Richard Boone*) *and
Draco* (*Dean Stockwell*), *arrives at his new
post.* (*Below*) *The Frisian Prince* (*Henry
Wilcoxon*) *in battle.* (The War Lord –
Universal)

early scenes needed reshooting and
clarifying. Surprisingly, Ava Gardner
proved most responsive to Guy Green's
direction and he completed the film
with little more trouble.

55 Days At Peking was an enthralling, sprawling ball of an adventure,
though it proved pale in terms of drama
compared to *Roman Empire.* Heston's
Matt Lewis was a poorly defined
character and had he chosen to play
Livius he could have made something
wonderful out of it.

When looking at *El Cid* and *55 Days
At Peking,* and then Heston's epics
that followed, *The War Lord* and
Khartoum, there is one major theme
running through them all. In every one
Heston played a leader of men besieged,
whether it was in a city (as in *El Cid*
and *Khartoum*), a barracks (*55 Days At
Peking*) or just a medieval tower (*The
War Lord*).

The War Lord is a prime example of
how the studios can wield so much
power that they can take a potential
masterpiece and turn it into something
mediocre, or, as in this case, a fine film
that fell short of its mark. Basically,
it was Heston's own production. He
first became interested in the film in
1962. It was based on a play called "The
Lovers" which had been submitted to
Chuck to play on Broadway a few
years earlier. He had turned it down,
but the play still fascinated him and
now he wanted to buy the screen rights,
which he did. He then got producer
Walter Selzter interested in the project.
Both men agreed it should *not* be an
epic.

"We should advertise it with 'A
Cast of Dozens,' " said Heston to
Seltzer.

They spent the best parts of 1962 and
1963 in getting a satisfactory script
and two days after the Christmas of
1963 Universal agreed to back them.
By now they had decided to call the film
The War Lord, since it conjured up
more of an image of a Norman knight
demanding his rights by taking somebody else's bride on her wedding night,
than *The Lovers.*

On September 14, 1964, with Frank
Schaffner ready to direct, Chuck check-
ed into his *War Lord* office at Universal.
On the door was the sign "Fraser
Productions" (Fraser being his son's
name). There were some problems on
casting. Richard Boone was fixed to
play Bors, but Universal didn't like

the idea of Stanley Baker for Draco
(who would have been perfect). The
biggest problem was in finding a leading lady.

Diane Baker was tested and turned
down. Universal came up with three
of their contract girls. All proved
negative, but Universal's contract
player Dean Stockwell ended up a wise
choice for Draco. Then they had another
look at the three Universal girls. They
chose Rosemary Forsyth.

Heston, in his capacity as creative
producer, had a strange experience
when he interviewed Henry Wilcoxon
for the Frisian Prince. There was once
a time when Wilcoxon stood on

DeMille's side of the desk and Heston
on the other. Now the roles were
reversed and Wilcoxon was hired by
Heston.

Next there was a wrangle with
Universal over how nude Rosemary
Forsyth should be. I always thought
nude was nude. Anyway, it was a problem, and the first of many with Universal.

Heston wanted to shoot in England.
Instead he had to be satisfied with
some marshes in northern California.
Chuck and Schaffner seemed pleased
with the way Rosemary was throwing
herself into the role. Then it was back
to Universal where they had built the

104

(*Top*) *Rosemary Forsyth's controversial nude scene.* (*Middle*) *Bronwyn,* (*Rosemary Forsyth*) *spends her first night of marriage with another man, Chrysagon.* (*Bottom*) *Chrysagon bears the tortuous healing process.* (The War Lord — *Universal*)

interiors of the tower on a sound stage and the exterior as a complete replica on the back lot.

The first rough cut of *The War Lord* ran nearly three hours. Part of the agreement with Universal was that it should run two. Heston and Schaffner felt the battles were too long. But this version came the closest to what Schaffner and Heston had envisaged. Work to trim down the battles began.

Universal, though, didn't want the battles cut. They wanted an epic, and to ensure it finished as such, they fired Frank Schaffner. Some studio executive called Ernie Nims took over the editing. The problem was that Heston and Co. had agreed to deliver a film two hours long and so far they hadn't. Universal were at liberty to take over.

In Heston's view (and it was *his* film, for goodness sake) the cuts made were pointless, except to reduce the nude scene to "a series of peep-show tease shots."

Seltzer and Heston confronted Universal for three solid hours and Chuck seemed to have the idea that they had managed to get Universal to restore enough to get the film closer to the original conception. He was wrong. It went out on release the way Universal wanted it to. Still, looking at the movie in complete ignorance of what happened, *The War Lord* is a marvellous picture and, (sorry Chuck) a respectable *epic*.

It was towards the end of the filming of *The War Lord*, in the winter of 1965, when he read Robert Adrey's masterful screenplay for *Khartoum*. It was the story of General Gordon, the British hero who loved the Sudan and defended it against the fanatical followers of the Mahdi.

Heston was attracted first by the script, which he today maintains is one of the finest screenplays he has ever read, and by the challenge of playing an Englishman. He called Carol Reed and asked him if he'd direct it. (Reed had previously directed Heston in *The Agony And The Ecstasy*.) Reed said yes. The producer Julian Blaustein was pleased with the choice of director, but eventually Reed turned it down. Blaustein gave the job to Basil Dearden, about whom Heston had lots of reservations. He told me, "While *Khartoum* is a very good film, it is not a very well *directed* film."

(*Top Right*) General Gordon (*Charlton Heston*) prepares to meet his inevitable death. (*Above*) Even when not filming, Heston displayed a liking for the Sudanese that Gordon had. (Khartoum – *United Artists*)

(*Below right*) Lt Bromhead (*Michael Caine*) and Lt Chard (*Stanley Baker*) keeping stiff-upper-lips while the Zulus attack. (Zulu – *Paramount*)

Chuck's disappointment in the choice of director was overcome by the casting of Ralph Richardson as Prime Minister Gladstone and Laurence Olivier as the Mahdi.

Filming began on August 11, 1965 at Pinewood Studios. Heston noted that Deardon shot few close-ups, not a good method from an actor's point of view, but this could well be to do with the fact that the film was being shot for the Cinerama screen.

The location shooting took the cast and crew to Cairo where Egyptian management proved faulty. Transport seemed to get lost, water sometimes wasn't available, and one day even the Nile steamer didn't turn up when everyone else did. It finally appeared an hour and a half late.

Chuck celebrated his forty-first birthday dressed as Gordon and entering Khartoum to a tumultuous reception by thousands of Sudanese working as extras.

For Heston, playing Gordon proved to be a technically brilliant performance, because, not only did he put his usual superior talent to the fore, but he produced a perfectly sound English accent which few other Americans could manage. *Khartoum* did well in Britain, especially in its Cinerama Roadshowings, but in America the film did poorly. It's possible that Gordon meant nothing to them, despite the fact that a sort of national hero of their own was portraying him.

Khartoum, in presenting a moment from Britain's history, did not reflect a particularly glorious one. Gordon's death in his futile effort to save Khartoum was an acute embarrassment to the British, not just because of the defeat, but because they had originally sent him there "off the record" so to speak.

A more glorious episode depicting our fighting men of yesteryear was the basis for Britain's most outstanding epic, *Zulu*. Brilliantly acted by a large cast and frighteningly real as thousands of Zulu warriors besiege a handful of Welsh soldiers at Rork's Drift,

Zulu stands as a monument to the late Stanley Baker who not only starred but produced as well. It's also director Cy Enfield's best work, and had he directed the so-called prequel, *Zulu Dawn*, that might have been as great as its predecessor.

Baker and Enfield rightly chose to film *Zulu* in the Drakensberg Mountains in South Africa in the summer of 1963. There is only one place in all the world where you can find genuine Zulus, and that's in Zululand. Busloads of Zulus were transported from their land to these mountains, and as soon as Baker saw them, his heart sank.

"For some sequences we had to spray the desert with paint to get the desired colour effect."

"They looked absolutely nothing," was his comment. "Even those who normally wore blankets on the kraals had bought or borrowed trousers, because, I later learned, they didn't want us to think them primitive.

"But when we gave them leopard skins and assegais, they were suddenly transformed. They began leaping about and dancing like dervishes. Most of them had never held a real spear before and they were ecstatic.

"Only one of them had ever seen a film before so we sent for one to show them. It was an old Gene Autrey western and they loved it. They stamped and shouted and whistled, and when that was over they couldn't wait to get before the cameras."

As props men began handing out rifles to the Zulus, some of the tribesman became a little wary, thinking that maybe it was a trap of some kind. To ease their minds Baker explained what the rifles were for, and to prove they were loaded with blanks, he had someone shoot him in the chest.

To portray the 130 soldiers who defended Rork's Drift, besides the stars, were young South African National Servicemen lent to the company by the government. When they came to

(*Top*) The Zulus attack. (*Middle*) A Zulu woman teaches Stanley Baker the Zulu stamp. (*Bottom*) The thin red line. (Zulu – Paramount)

(*Top*) *The survivors of the Light Brigade.* (*Middle*) *Captain Nolan (*David Hemmings*) delivers the message for the Light Brigade to charge.* (*Bottom*) *Captain Morris (*Mark Burns*) fights for his life.* (The Charge of the Light Brigade – *United Artists*)

shoot the first battle scene the soldiers were distinctly lacking the zeal the Zulus seemed to have, and the Zulus won. According to the script the Zulus were supposed to be held back. So the soldiers had to be given some intensive training by their officers.

Among the stars at Rork's Drift were James Booth, Nigel Green, Jack Hawkins, Ulla Jacobson and a young Cockney actor just rising to the ranks of stardom, Michael Caine.

It was due to the efforts of his friend Stanley Baker that he won the role of the upper-crust officer. One day one of the production office secretaries found Michael and revealed to him that a telegram had arrived from the financiers (Caine himself told me this story but didn't mention exactly from whom the message came, but the man behind the money was Joe Levine) which said that they wanted him out of the picture.

"Stanley Baker refused to do it," said Michael. "He had faith in me, Cy had faith in me, but the people who produced the picture didn't. I had a seven year contract with Joe Levine, which, when the picture was finished, was dropped and given to James Booth."

Because of the 1957 South Africa Act that forbids any white man from having relationships with a black woman, punishable by seven years imprisonment, Stanley Baker impressed on his cast and crew the necessity for celibacy where the hundreds of black dancing girls seen in the first sequence were concerned.

As the girls lined up for their big scene in which they dance topless, Stanley Baker, Jack Hawkins and the others watched the beauty parade pass by.

"Steady lads," said Jack Hawkins. "There goes 700 years of hard labour!"

When the scene was completed two oxen were roasted on spits. The Zulus went wild. The crew had forgotten that in Zululand a cow is not so much meat as currency and few Zulus got the chance to eat meat. They all made short work of the meal.

There have been a number of epics about the British Empire and its heroes. There have also been films about its defeats. Tony Richardson's disturbing and magnificent *The Charge Of The Light Brigade* (1968) was almost *too* real in its depiction of the cruel,

almost servile treatment of enlisted men, and the distinct lack of glory in battle. He directed the famous charge itself in Turkey and enlisted a top-notch British cast with Trevor Howard, Vanessa Redgrave, John Gielgud, Harry Andrews, Jill Bennet and David Hemmings. There had been four other previous productions with the same title, including the famous Errol Flynn swashbuckler, but none could compare to this in terms of frightening reality. The charge was a blunder and Richardson shows that the British army at that time was full of blunderers. Even Lord Raglan, played with some humour by Gielgud, was a general of alarming senility. He knows there is a war *somewhere*. "I've got a map of it," he says, but can't find it. Into the room comes the only sane man in the film, Captain Nolan (Hemmings). "Have you got a map?" Raglan asks him.

Then there is Lord Cardigan (Trevor Howard) who is the first over the Russian line but "retires" from the battle immediately. Riding over the blood-stained field after the Light Brigade has been decimated, he inquires, "Anyone seen my regiment?"

Heroes, of course, are never shown in a bad light and one certainly didn't expect Richard Attenborough, in his capacity as a director, to do anything but justice to *Young Winston* Churchill, one of the few epics of the Seventies. But in this land of filmed heroes it is completely overshadowed by a film that was, I suppose, about a man who was more of a hero to his friends the Arabs than to his fellow British – *Lawrence Of Arabia*.

Producer Sam Spiegel and director David Lean had been looking for a further vehicle ever since their triumphant collaboration on *The Bridge On The River Kwai* in 1957. Their first idea was to film the life and death of Mahatma Ghandi, but abandoned the idea realising they would be tampering with a man who was a saint to his followers. Neither Spiegel nor Lean knew how to approach such a subject without seeming presumptuous.

Spiegel had first read T. E. Lawrence's own account of his Arabian experiences, "Seven Pillars Of Widsom",

(*Right*) *Some of the distinguished cast of* Lawrence Of Arabia: *Peter O' Toole, Alec Guinness, Claude Rains, Anthony Quale and Jack Hawkins.* (*Below*) *Anthony Quinn as Auda Abu Tayi.* (*Bottom right*) *Alec Guinness as Prince Feisal.* (Lawrence Of Arabia – *Columbia*)

(Above) Led by Sherif Ali (Omar Sharif), Lawrence comes to the camp of Prince Feisal. (Top right) Lawrence in Auda's camp. (Right) Auda's first meeting with Lawrence. (Lawrence Of Arabia—Columbia)

some years before its general publication. By 1962 the film rights had become available and Spiegel immediately acquired them. It was while in India deciding which way to go on the Ghandi project that Spiegel and Lean decided to film *Lawrence Of Arabia*. They engaged British playwright Robert Bolt to write the screenplay and then set about the task of finding their Lawrence.

They decided to find an "unknown" for the role and surround him with names. The part eventually fell to young Irish actor Peter O'Toole who was so brilliant in the film that it's unlikely that anyone could ever do the role as much justice if ever another version is made. O'Toole, determined to get deep into the man's soul, read the book so many times he was able to recite long passages from it by heart, studied the man's life and learned about Arabian folk lore.

He found himself in distinguished company: Alec Guinness as Prince Feisal, Anthony Quinn as the Howeitat sheikh, Auda Abu Tayi, Jack Hawkins as Allenby, Lawrence's commander-in-chief, Claude Rains as Allenby's devious political advisor Dryden, Jose Ferrer, superb as the homosexual and cruel Turkish bey, Anthony Quayle as Colonel Brighton, and Arthur Kennedy as the newspaperman, Bentley. Millions of female hearts were sent fluttering by the arrival on screen of Omar Sharif as Sheik Ali ibn el Kharish. The first appearance of Kharish,

riding out of a haze, is still especially to the ladies, one of the film's most memorable moments. Sadly, that was not Sharif riding the camel but his stand-in.

In his search for suitable locations, Lean went to Jordan with Art Director John Box, and there in the desert they found the wreckage of trains blown up by Lawrence nearly forty years beforehand. King Hussein, descendant of Hussein of Mecca, Prince Feisal's father, gave Spiegel and Lean help in making the film as well as his protection.

Some scenes had to be filmed in other countries. Cairo, Damascus and Jerusalem looked too modern, so Lean took

his unit to Spain and filmed at Seville where the Moorish-Arabic architecture gave the required effect. Akaba was completely recreated in Spain with a Turkish camp alongside it. Heavily involved with the structural side of the filming was Vic Simpson who told me, "I spent two years on *Lawrence* as Master Painter, covering the whole scenic side of the picture. You may not believe this but there were several sequences for which we had to spray the desert with paint to get the desired colour effect."

The film itself, no matter how stupendous it was visually, would certainly have been incomplete without its wonderful score by Maurice

Jarre, who again worked for Lean on *Doctor Zhivago* and *Ryan's Daughter*.

Recalls Jarre; "I enjoyed doing *Lawrence* even more than *Zhivago*. Actually, I was the third choice for *Lawrence*. One well-known composer wanted a year's contract in which to compose the music. I wrote the entire score in four weeks – and that won me my first Oscar."

(Far right) Christopher Plummer as the Duke of Wellington. (Below) A cavalry charge. (Bottom) The battleground at Waterloo. (Waterloo – Columbia)

When it comes to pure logistics, one of the biggest productions about the British Empire, and in this instance a glorious British victory, is Dino De Laurentiis' production *Waterloo*. Besides having an expensive cast including Rod Steiger as Napoleon, Christopher Plummer as Wellington, Orson Welles as Louis XVIII, plus Jack Hawkins (again?), Virginia McKenna and Rupert Davies, *Waterloo* boasted nearly 20,000 soldiers of the Red Army to portray British and French troops. The cost of the film came to over £12,000,000 and would have cost more had it been filmed in the West.

Instead, it was filmed in the Ukraine by director Sergei Bondarchuk, one of Russia's foremost movie-makers.

Strangely enough, both Laurentiis and Bondarchuck each made their own versions of another famous Napoleonic saga, *War And Peace*.

Laurentiis made his American-Italian co-production in 1956 with King Vidor directing and starring Henry Fonda, Audrey Hepburn and Mel Ferrer. In the role of Napoleon was Herbert Lom who had also portrayed the French Emperor in the movie *The Young Mr. Pitt* in 1941 as well as on stage in "Betzi".

"Could you spare 20 minutes Mr Lom; two hundred French officers want to meet Napoleon?"

The two versions of War And Peace:
(Below) the American-Italian co-production.
(Bottom) the Russian epic.

Lom recalls; "When we were filming *War And Peace* in Italy we had thousands of troops playing Russians and Frenchmen for the battle scenes. They refused to use cardboard swords and insisted on using real ones.

"I arrived on the set one morning dressed as Napoleon and the first assistant director came to me and said, '*Could you spare twenty minutes, Mr. Lom?*' He pointed to a queue of about two hundred men and this assistant director said, '*They all want to meet Napoleon.*' I said, '*You're joking.*' He said, '*No, no. They're all officers, and they've expressed a desire to meet you and shake your hand.*' So in my Berman's uniform I had to stand there and shake every one of them by the hand, and keep my expression very serious. They were clicking their heels, and with great respect they all shook hands with Napoleon.

"I can remember King Vidor (who

was then in his sixties) playing the guitar after dinner. I remember once overhearing a conversation between him and Hank Fonda. Hank was objecting to a line in the script, and he said, 'Gee, I can't say that. It doesn't feel real.' Vidor said, 'Of course it isn't real. It's a movie!' "

Vidor had a point! Nothing much about the film was real. Americans played Russians. Italy portrayed Russia. Still, it looked real even if not all the performances did.

When it came to the Russian version of *War And Peace* there was no substituting Russians for foreigners and Russia for some alien land. The whole cast and crew were Russian and it was filmed in their beloved home land.

Sergei Bondarchuk produced, directed and starred, not to mention adding his own words to the screenplay. It's undoubtedly the most expensive film ever made, costing 100,000,000 dollars. The battle of Borodino is probably the most awesome battle ever photo-

graphed, as 120,000 Soviet soldiers swarm over the screen portraying the Russian and French troops.

Being filmed in Russia, where there is no such law as there is in most other

(*Below left*) *Panic spreads through Moscow when news of Napoleon's advance on the city reaches there. (Below) Mel Ferrer and Oskar Homolka at the head of hundreds of Italians all playing Russians. (Bottom) The Russian army. (War And Peace — Paramount)*

(*Above*) *The Russian army salute their royal family.* (Nicholas And Alexandra — *Columbia*)

(*Right*) *Yuri* (*Omar Sharif*) *is caught up in the revolution.* (*Bottom*) *Alexander* (*Ralph Richardson*) *and Anna* (*Siobhan McKenna*) *rear the orphan Yuri* (*Tarek Sharif*). (Doctor Zhivago — *MGM*)

countries forbidding the use of trip wires to cause horses to fall, animals were, I suspect, put at risk, notably the horses in the spectacular charges, although there is nothing to confirm that there were casualties. But I did learn from various members of Columbia's publicity department that some 400 horses were killed while filming the Charge of the Scott's greys in *Waterloo* because trip wires were used. And remember, *Waterloo* and *War And Peace* were both directed by Bondarchuk and both were filmed in Russia where regard for animal life seems to be sadly lacking.

For non-Russian productions about that country, other locations have to be found. Sam Spiegel filmed his non-spectacular yet lavishly mounted *Nicholas And Alexandra* in Spain utilising much of the same talent to help recreate Russia that his ex-collaborator David

(*Above*) *Yuri and Lara (Julie Christie) do what they can for the wounded.* (*Top right*) *Komarovsky (Rod Steiger) and Lara (Julie Christie) in her mother's dressmaking establishment.* (*Right*) *Thousands of deserters leave the front during World War 1.* (Doctor Zhivago — *MGM*)

Lean had used in *Doctor Zhivago*, namely director of photography Freddie Young and production designer John Box, the man most responsible for rebuilding Moscow twice for both films.

Box's masterpiece actually was his Moscow for *Zhivago* which was built in Madrid. The set included a half-mile long street with hundreds of shops, a tram line and trolley cars, a side street leading to a factory, the Red Square and dominating it all, the Kremlin.

Lean filled his cast with many stars, including two from *Lawrence Of Arabia;* Omar Sharif in the title role, and Alec Guinness. There was also Rod Steiger, Julie Christie, Ralph Richardson, Tom Courteney, Siobhan McKenna and Geraldine Chaplin.

Sir Alec's inclusion doesn't come to any as a great surprise . . . except maybe to himself. He says, "I didn't expect to be in it. I had tried to read the book and failed; all those Russian names baffled me. I didn't find out what it was all about until I read the script, to be quite honest.

"When the project was first announced David Lean said, '*I don't want any prissy English ladies and gentlemen in this.*' So to find Ralph Richardson and myself promptly engaged was something of a surprise. David prefers

(*Above*) *Taras* (*Yul Brynner*) *and his son Andrei* (*Tony Curtis*) *at the head of the Cossacks.* (*Right*) *Yul Brynner off-set during filming of* Taras Bulba (*United Artists*)

American actors to British ones, He really thinks we are a bit prissy."

As great as *Doctor Zhivago* may have been, as successful as it was and as deserving as it was of its 5 Oscars, *the* classic Russian story for me has to be the Gogol classic, *Taras Bulba*, filmed in 1962.

Here again I'm probably alone in praising this film, at least among my colleagues I suspect, while I know that the film is a great favourite among those who have seen it either at the cinema or on television. The director J. Lee Thompson revealed to me that the original idea was to film a $2\frac{1}{2}$–3 hour Roadshow. I'll never know for sure what the original conception was like because when news came through that Roadshows were no longer popular, the film was cut down to two hours.

The two stars, Yul Brynner and Tony Curtis, suddenly found some of their more dramatic moments completely

(Above) On screen lovers Natalia and Andrei became off-screen lovers Christine Kaufmann and Tony Curtis. (Top right) Tony and daughter Jamie, in between scenes of Taras Bulba. (Bottom right) The battle for Dubno from Taras Bulba (United Artists).

missing. "Tony had some brilliant scenes, that ended up on the cutting room floor," Thompson told me, "So did Yul. To this day Yul blames me for ruining his performance."

I wouldn't have said Brynner's performance was ruined (but then I never saw the *whole* film), because for me he has never been better. Dressed in great baggy pants with a scalp lock flowing from his bald head and slicing the air with a Cossack sabre, Brynner looked like he had stepped out of history. As the Cossack Colonel he was ruthless. As the father of two devoted sons (Tony Curtis and Perry Lopez) he was movingly loving.

For Tony Curtis it was something of a return to the swashing of buckles as he had done in his early career in films like *The Prince Who Was A Thief* and *The Black Shield Of Falworth*. But there were also echoes of the Curtis who proved what a superb actor he is in *The Defiant Ones* and *Trapeze*. *Taras Bulba* was made at a time when Curtis had a strong phobia about flying, and when it came to making the long journey to Argentina where the

(*Top*) *The Poles are caught in a surprise attack by the Cossacks.* (*Right*) *Andrei and Natalia try to escape the city on the roof of a wagon carrying plague victims.* (*Bottom*) *Taras mourns the death of Andrei. "This is now Cossack soil — we'll bury him here."* (*Opposite*) *The Polish army await the arrival of the Cossacks outside Dubno.* (*Taras Bulba* — *United Artists*)

film was shot, he went along by boat while wife Janet Leigh flew.

Producer Harold Hecht, who chose to shoot in and around the rugged foothills of the snow-capped Andes, hired 10,000 Gauchos and their horses to charge about as the splendid Cossack army. To play the Turks and the Poles, Hecht enlisted 1,000 Argentine Cavalry.

American actor Sam Wanamaker, who was so watchable as another of the Cossack colonels, prepared himself for the role by playing at Cossacks at Goring-by-sea in England. Twice a day, with his moustache and beard fully grown for his role, Wanamaker would mount his high-spirited white mare and gallop like hell over the sands, howling like crazy at the top of his voice. The conservative locals were naturally surprised by such erratic behaviour and were heard to point out, "Well, he *is* American, my dear."

Providing the female interest was 17-year-old Christine Kaufmann as a Polish noble who captures the heart of the younger Bulba, played by Tony Curtis. Curtis' marriage to Janet was all but over and he found new adventure and romance with his leading lady. It was soon obvious to everyone that the two had fallen in love. Many blamed Christine for the break-up of Tony's marriage to Janet, but that was already just about over. When *Taras Bulba* was finally in the can Tony and

Christine became man and wife, a marriage destined for the divorce courts. But that's another story.

When I interviewed Tony I was surprised to find that he too thought it was a good movie. He told me:

"I liked working with Yul very much, I really did. I liked that picture very much, although it got a little out of hand in the making. J. Lee Thompson and the producer Harold Hecht produced a great deal of tension on the set. My marriage was splitting up then and I was in a very close . . . . er . . . . proximity with Christine which bore unnecessary strains on everybody. It provoked relationships that shouldn't have been provoked and vice-versa. That picture is a haze to me, it was so tough to make. Oh, *tough!* We went down to South Argentina, we did all that stuff, went all the way back to California to finish it up.

"I like the film. It's got some exquisite moments, really moving moments when that father confronts his son. God, I'll never forget that moment when he shoots him. All you know of it is the little hole in the breastplate. Wasn't that incredible? I've never seen that on the screen before. Usually you see people smeared in blood, yet all you see is a tiny, clear little hole. Wow!

"It was a great part for Yul. It was right down his alley, right out of his background."

Meanwhile, back in Argentina J. Lee Thompson was preparing to shoot the big, final battle in which hundreds of men and horses pitch over the side of a cliff. The shot of these figures falling

(*Above*) *Andrei dances with a gypsy.*
(Taras Bulba — *United Artists*)

(*Right*) *Yul Brynner and George Chakiris in*
(Kings Of The Sun — *United Artists*).

into the ravine is a horribly impressive moment, it looks so realistic. I asked Thompson if the horses seen falling were real or just dummies?

"They were dummies," he said. "But the frightening thing is these riders said to me, '*If you want, we'll ride them over the edge.*' It didn't bother them if a couple of hundred horses were slaughtered. I said, '*No, we'll use dummies.*' And they looked just as real."

It's difficult to gauge Yul Brynner's own reaction to the movie. He once related how Thompson rung him from a reception following the screening of the film. Thompson, according to Brynner, was drunk, and said, "Yul, I've just watched the movie again, and I really don't see why you had to shoot Tony."

It may well have been Thompson's idea of a joke, but it hit Brynner hard. "After that the film lost all credibility for me," he said.

Still, Brynner did make another film almost immediately after for J. Lee Thompson. This was *Kings Of The Sun*, a weak tale of how the Mayans come to settle in North America and face danger from a tribe of savage Indians. George Chakiris was the Mayan king and Yul Brynner was the splendid warrior Black Eagle.

Long ships, high seas and mutinous Marlon

Such roles put Yul Brynner firmly in the barbarian-type casting slot, and in 1965 he was offered the role of *Genghis Khan* by producer Irving Allen. Brynner rejected the part when Allen refused to meet his astronomical fee, and the part went to relative newcomer Omar Sharif. Here again, I stand very much alone in my profession in thinking that *Genghis Khan* was a fantastic piece of screen entertainment. Admittedly, some of the casting was somewhat erratic. James Mason and Robert Morley don't really make ideal Chinamen, but Eli Wallach as the Persian Shah added some light relief with intended humour and Stephen Boyd as the Khan's deadly enemy Jamuga was enjoyably evil. Omar Sharif was probably better casting anyway than Yul Brynner because Genghis Khan is seen first as a young man and then gradually ages. Sharif is even seen briefly at the beginning

(Left) Bortei (Francoise Dorleac) and Temujin (Omar Sharif), before he becomes the Genghis Khan. (Bottom left) At first, Temujin's band is made up of only two other Mongols (Michael Horden and Woody Strode). (Below) Jamuga (Stephen Boyd) kidnaps Bortie. (Genghis Khan—Columbia)

playing the Khan's father. As the Khan's irresistible wife was the fated François Dorleac, the French actress who, just two years later, died in a car crash.

Genghis Khan was certainly an improvement on Allen's previous epic, *The Long Ships*, a Viking saga that failed to match Kirk Douglas' own production of 1958, *The Vikings*. Some inspired casting went into *The Vikings*,

directed by Richard Fleischer who, like Stanley Kubrick two years later, had to put his employer, Kirk Douglas, through his paces, but as yet I've heard no complaints from Fleischer. Douglas was not the hero, this time, but not exactly the heavy either. Our gallant hero was a bearded Tony Curtis and the heroine, Janet Leigh. It was not a humorous role for Curtis, but a gritty, and often uncomfortable part.

In one scene he is left to drown in a freezing rock pool while in another he has his hand cut off.

There was some strange casting for *The Long Ships*, starring Richard Widmark as a Viking adventurer, Sidney Poitier as his Moorish adversary, and Russ Tamblyn adding some comedy relief. At least, I *hope* that was his intention.

The Vikings and *The Long Ships* have one thing in common, besides the subject matter, and that is Jack Cardiff. On the earlier film he was the director of photography while on Irving Allen's film he was promoted to director.

"I didn't want to do *The Long Ships* because I'd already worked on *The Vikings* and I knew all the terrible problems," he told me. "With *The Vikings* we worked in Norway and we had these boats in the narrow fjords going in various directions. I remember

(Left) Temujin defeats Jamuga (Stephen Boud) but is fatally wounded. (Bottom) Bortei mourns the death of Temujin. (Genghis Khan — Columbia)

(Opposite top left) One of The Long Ships. (Top right) Two unlikely Vikings, Russ Tamblyn and Richard Widmark, find the Golden Bell. (Bottom) The African Moors, with their Viking slaves, bring back the famous Golden Bell. (The Long Ships — Columbia)

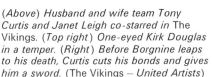

(*Above*) *Husband and wife team Tony Curtis and Janet Leigh co-starred in* The Vikings. (*Top right*) *One-eyed Kirk Douglas in a temper.* (*Right*) *Before Borgnine leaps to his death, Curtis cuts his bonds and gives him a sword.* (The Vikings – *United Artists*)

(*Opposite top*) *Russ Tamblyn swashes his buckle with Sidney Poitier.* (The Long Ships – *Columbia*)

(*Opposite bottom*) *Tony Curtis, Kirk Douglas, Ernest Borgnine and James Donald in* The Vikings (*United Artists*)

one fantastic shot, a long shot of the viking ships coming up the fjords and they were driven by motors. The wind was in the wrong direction and the sails were billowing the wrong way. It was the funniest thing to see a ship going forward with the sail going the other way.

"When we got to Norway we had a lot of bad weather and I persuaded Kirk Douglas that we could shoot in the rain and so after that we shot *everything* in the rain. It wasn't a long picture. We spent about three or four months on it and it was a lot of fun.

"*The Long Ships* was also about three or four months. It was a more lavish picture and we had all that stuff with the Golden Bell and we travelled around the world much more. It turned out to be more of a comedy picture after all because you can't really take those sort of things too seriously. I think if it had been done in the right way with big tough Norwegians, it would have made all the difference. But when you've got a mixed cast it never quite rings as it should do."

When it comes to sea-going sagas

the one that has to stand out as being the most famous, the most adventurous and the most jinxed is the 1962 MGM make of *Mutiny On The Bounty.*

Aaron Rosenberg was the producer who, like Walter Wanger with *Cleopatra,* would probably have never started the project had he known how unkindly fate would treat it. Rosenberg commissioned Eric Ambler to write the script and when that was completed it was sent to Marlon Brando to read.

"He didn't like the script," says Rosenberg. "He said he wanted to play Fletcher Christian, but he didn't like the ending of the picture. He wanted a long sequence on Pitcairn Island to be included."

Two other writers reshaped the script; Borden Chase and William

Driskill. Brando still wasn't happy and had a go at writing his own. Rosenberg read Brando's version and rejected it.

"All right," said Brando. "But you're making the biggest mistake of your life. You've made nothing but mistakes since the picture started. If this is what you want, this is what you're going to get. I'll just do anything I'm told."

The film began shooting in 1960 under the direction of Carol Reed. When Reed and Rosenberg clashed over their different concepts of Bligh's character, the director quit. Lewis Milestone took over and found Brando unhappy about everything. The script was still being fashioned and Brando, who had been given a vast amount of artistic control, found himself up against a wall when trying to put forward his ideas to Reed. Consequently, Brando chose not to do as Milestone wanted him to do. The star was also proving himself unpopular with Trevor Howard, who played Captain Bligh, and the rest of the cast. But if Brando was proving difficult it probably had more to do with the fact that he wasn't being given the artistic control Rosenberg had promised him. However, blame for the film's problems have always been attributed, perhaps unfairly, to Brando.

"I knew we were going to have a stormy passage right away," Milestone says of his relationship, with Brando. "I like to get on with things, but Brando likes to discuss every scene, every line for hours. I felt enough time had been wasted but time didn't seem to mean anything to Brando. After a lot of bad feeling, the next thing I knew was Rosenberg was on the set every day and Brando was arguing about every scene with *him* instead of me. When eventually the arguments were over, I'd be told Brando was ready for the cameras. It was a terrible way to make a picture."

By the time the picture was half finished Milestone was no longer directing Brando. He just dealt with the other actors and, when it was time to shoot, Milestone would simply put up his feet, call for 'Action! Camera!' and let Brando deal with the scene himself.

The budget finally came home at a then staggering nine million pounds, two million of which Milestone blames on Brando.

"Instead of boarding the ship at the dock, like everyone else," says the director, "Brando insisted on a speedboat to take him out to the ship when we were at sea. Three weeks before we were due to leave Tahiti he decided to move from the house he had to an abandoned villa some thirty miles away. It cost us more than £2,000 to make it habitable for him for the week or two he lived in it."

Today Trevor Howard is speechless when asked about Brando, and Richard Harris who co-starred, says he would never make another film with Brando.

Many critics feel that this Techni-

(Below) Trevor Howard, so superb as Captain Bligh. (Mutiny On The Bounty – MGM)

(Opposite top) The Bounty gets a warm reception. (Opposite bottom) Another on-screen affair that continued off-screen: Marlon Brando and Tarita. (Mutiny On The Bounty – MGM)

colored and wide-screened version is inferior to the 1935 black and white classic which cast Charles Laughton as Bligh and Clark Gable as an Americanised Fletcher Christian. Frankly, I'd disagree, although this is not to detract from the original version's excellence. The two pictures, though with the same subject, are two very different types of films. The original was more of a romantic adventure while the remake was far more gritty (or should it be salty?), a lot more spectacular and the actual mutiny itself far more dramatic.

What the original had going for it was a totally ruthless Laughton and a superbly masculine and heroic Gable. Actually, Laughton steals the film and Gable had to wait just a few more years before he was able to dominate a true epic, and certainly one of the greatest ever made.

(*Right and below*) *Scenes from the 1935 version of* Mutiny On The Bounty *which starred Clark Gable as Fletcher Christian and Charles Laughton as Captain Bligh.* (*MGM*)

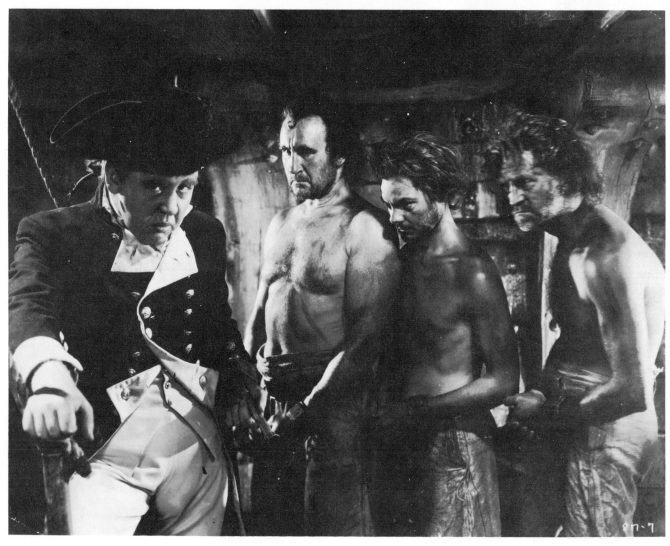

(Above) Samuel Bronston's three
dimensional set for 55 Days In Peking

(Centre) After taking Akaba, Lawrence
(Peter O'Toole) returns to British H.Q.
(Left) Lawrence at the head of a camel
corps. (Lawrence of Arabia – Columbia)

Henry Fonda, Audrey Hepburn and Mel Ferrer starred in War and Peace (*Paramount*).

The battle of Waterloo (*Columbia*).

(*Above*) Lara (*Julie Christie*) and Yuri
(*Omar Sharif*). (*Left*) John Box's splendid
recreation of Moscow for Doctor Zhivago
(*MGM*)

(Above) Sherman (John Wayne) tries to dissuade Grant (Henry Morgan) from quitting. (Left) The Buffaloes pummel a railroad camp. (How the West Was Won – MGM – Cinerama)

(Opposite top) The carnage of civil war. (Opposite bottom) Rhett (Clark Gable) consoles the recently widowed Scarlett (Vivien Leigh) at the ball. (Gone with the Wind – MGM)

Einar (*Kirk Douglas*) *is popular among his own Viking people.* (The Vikings — *United Artists*).

Einar and Ragnar (*Ernest Borgnine*) *have an unwilling passenger, Morgana* (*Janet Leigh*). (The Vikings — *United Artists*).

"Don't give me all that manure about art; I'm up to my shoulders trying to get this picture together."

Gone With The Wind.

Vivien Leigh wanted desperately to play Scarlett O'Hara.

Clark Gable was one of the very few convinced he was not ideal to play Rhett Butler. Gable was 38 when he played Butler, and his casting by producer David O. Selznick helped to make Metro-Goldwyn-Mayer a whole lot richer than they already were since Gable was one of their contract stars and Selznick had to give MGM distribution rights and 50 per cent of the profits.

While Selznick was signing the deal with Louis B. Mayer he was still searching for his Scarlett O'Hara. The story of how Vivien Leigh won the part – when she was led to Selznick's chair from where he watched them burning Atlanta and was told, "Meet your Scarlett O'Hara!" by his brother Myron – has been over simplified by time. It did happen that way, but Vivien didn't win the part there and then. She had to be tested.

She turned up on the day of her test to find other actresses also eager for the part. The first to be tested was Jean Arthur. She locked herself in the dressing room and had to be coaxed out by the director George Cukor. Then came Joan Bennett whose test, according to the rumour that swiftly spread throughout the studio, was great.

Finally it was Vivien's turn. Leslie Howard was there to play Ashley Wilkes and after the test he admitted to Vivien that he had never read the book and detested Ashley for being a weak, wet character. He'd accepted the role because Selznick was very persuasive, especially with a cheque book.

Cukor made no sign of favouritism to any of the tested actresses and all he said to Vivien was, "Thank you, Vivien, that was fine."

On Christmas day, 1938, Vivien and her husband Laurence Olivier were invited to Cukor's home where other contestants for the role awaited news

Following their escape from war-torn Atlanta, Rhett Butler (Clark Gable) bids farewell to Scarlett (Vivien Leigh). (Gone With The Wind – MGM)

of his choice. Paulette Goddard seemed to be well in the running. Vivien thought she no longer stood a chance. Other members of the cast were there and Cukor introduced Vivien and Olivier to all of them. Then he drew Vivien over to a quiet corner and said, "Well, it's all settled. David has made his choice."

Being very brave, Vivien said, "That must be a relief for you."

"Oh, *vastly* relieved," he replied, and added, "I guess we're stuck with you."

In the very early stages of production, Vivien realised that Gable was uncomfortable in his role and that he was especially displeased with Cukor who had a reputation for being a "woman's director." Also, Selznick was himself becoming dissatisfied with the direct-

(*Left*) *The first scene filmed; the burning of Atlanta.* (*Below*) *Scarlett walks among the wounded.* (*Opposite*) *Even while Atlanta burns, Rhett keeps cool.* (Gone With The Wind – *MGM*)

or's concern with authenticity rather than the scope and sweep of history.

Gable revealed his insecurity and Selznick made his visits to the set more consistently. Still unhappy, Gable started refusing to show up and at first Cukor shot around him. On the thirteenth of February Selznick fired Cukor. Vivien Leigh and Olivia De Havilland (playing Melanie) were horror-struck. They went straight to Selznick's office and wept real tears in defence of Cukor. All to no avail. They became practical and said that only Cukor knew what kind of a film he was making because the script was far from being satisfactorily completed. Selznick had to confess that while he too loved Cukor he had to put the film's interest first. The new director was Victor Fleming, Gable's favourite director and pal.

However, Cukor continued to direct the ladies' performances. Both Vivien and Olivia had secret meetings with George who helped them far more than Fleming, who only ever advised, "Ham it up."

The cast never caused any trouble for Fleming because they were all too

(*Above*) *Scarlett is caught up in the tide of panic in Atlanta's streets, but* (*bottom picture*) *is rescued by Rhett.* (Gone With The Wind – *MGM*)

concerned with getting the picture finished. But one day, when Vivien told him he should really read the book, he told her to "shove it up her Royal British ass" and then went home and got drunk. Later, Vivien, Gable and Selznick arrived at Fleming's house with a cage of lovebirds, a peace offering.

Eventually, Fleming found himself on the verge of a nervous breakdown. While he would direct one day, Sam Wood directed the next. Finally, *almost* finally, Sam Wood was directing solo, but Selznick was dissatisfied. He directed the final sequence himself. In fact, he did two versions of Gable's last line, "Frankly, my dear, I don't give a damn," because the censors objected to the

word "damn," and so Selznick changed it to, "Frankly, my dear, I don't care." It was, of course, the original that was finally used.

The film had also taken its toll on Vivien. She was completely drained and lost a tremendous amount of weight. When Selznick wanted to completely reshoot the opening sequence he took one look at Vivien and realised that she looked far too diminished for the fresh, lively Scarlett that opens the film. He postponed the filming for a month to allow her to rest. However, the scene never was re-shot and *Gone With The Wind* was finally in the can.

During the reconstruction period, Ashley (Leslie Howard) helps Scarlett to rebuild the plantation on Tara. (Below) Ashley's not-so-happy birthday party. Wife Melanie (Olivia De Havilland) is present but not sweetheart Scarlett. (Gone With The Wind — MGM)

Gone With The Wind was never really an authentic film about the history of the New World. It did have some impressive scenes that gave an idea what conditions the American Civil War brought to soldiers and citizens alike. Sergio Leone did more to bring us closer to a truer feeling of the Civil War in *The Good, The Bad And The Ugly* by basing his battle, trenches and POW camp scenes on actual photographs of the period.

Probably the most famous of all the Civil War pictures is D. W. Griffith's *The Birth Of A Nation*. Originally called *The Clansman*, the movie was a one-sided view of the war that glorified the Klu Klux Klan. Griffith directed the

(*Top and below*) *The American Civil War as seen by director D. W. Griffith in* The Birth Of A Nation.

(*Opposite*) *The awesome Babylon scene from Griffith's* Intolerance.

film without a script. It took six months to film and only one day was spent shooting the Battle of Petersburg in San Fernando Valley. It cost 85,000 dollars and to finish the project Griffith had to sell everything he owned.

Filmed in 1915, liberal audiences of that day almost rioted at screenings, while many survivors of the war were seen crying at the memories it evoked.

(It's worth digressing here briefly from the American Historical film to discuss D. W. Griffith's intended successor to *Birth Of A Nation* – *Intolerance*. It was after his great Civil War masterpiece that Griffith poured all his artistic and financial resources into this truly mammoth production which is perhaps the ultimate epic with its multi-faceted plot. It included the Crucifixion of Christ, the Saint Bartolomew's Day Bloodbath and of course the famous fall of Babylon which featured the most recognised giant set of all time.

The city of Babylon stood 90 feet, overlooking Sunset Boulevard and the

elephants that sat atop the walls looking out over Hollywood were about thirty feet high.)

There have been few actual historical films about America that could be called epics. There have of course been innumerable westerns, but how many belong in this book? The first and foremost that is always in my mind, and one that really is a period film rather than a western, is John Wayne's *The Alamo*.

Critics love pulling this wonderful and inspiring film apart, probably because it was John Wayne's first attempt at directing. He also produced and starred as Davy Crockett. In terms of what Wayne gave to the world, *The Alamo* is his most important work. No other film has ever portrayed courage so movingly as in this great story of how 185 Americans defended the broken down mission known as the Alamo against 5,000 Mexican troops led by the dictator Santa Anna.

John Ford's stamp on Wayne is more than evident in the film, parti-

cularly in its sentimentality and lyrical dialogue. Wayne no doubt also leaned towards his friend and favourite director in his visual concept. The first sight of Crockett and his Tennesseeans coming through the long grass with the camera tilted upwards, showed that Wayne had certainly captured the poetic mood of Ford.

John Ford was in fact in on the production right from its early stages, advising Wayne in his choice of stars and later directing a couple of scenes for the film that were sadly cut out. When Laurence Harvey arrived in America and nervously faced Wayne who was interested in the English actor for the role of Colonel William Barret Travis, he immediately related his experiences and accomplishments at Stratford and the Old Vic.

To his great and gentlemanly amazement, Wayne growled, "Don't give me all that manure about art. I'm up to my shoulders trying to get this picture together."

Sitting behind a black patch over one

eye was John Ford who told the Duke, "We haven't got much time. Just sign him up."

Richard Widmark as Colonel James Bowie was brilliant and his style of humour and rugged outdoor image played off perfectly against Wayne's own attributes. Also in the film were pop star Frankie Avalon, Wayne's son Patrick, beautiful Mexican actress Linda Cristal, Joan O'Brien, Chill Wills and one of the cinema's finest second fiddle players, Ken Curtis. Making her film debut was Wayne's daughter Aissa as the daughter of Joan O'Brien and Curtis.

Ever since he started his own production company, Batjac, Wayne wanted to film *The Alamo*. At one time he actually started production in Mexico but after a month he abandoned it due to the excessive cost.

Wayne estimated that the film would probably cost 6–8,000,000 dollars. He had a contract to do some films for United Artists and they came up with some of the capital, allowing Wayne to re-start his pet project. In October, 1957 he finally went into action with *The Alamo* in Bracketville, Texas, where art director Al Ybarra construct-ed a replica of the mission turned fortress, part of which still stands today as a monument to the Alamo's defenders.

Shooting didn't actually begin until 1960 and it must have been due only to God's help and Wayne's enthusiasm that he managed to survive the task of producing, directing and starring in a film of such magnitude.

There were many moments when Wayne must have wondered what the hell he thought he was doing shouldering all the responsibility himself. He never enjoyed a social life throughout production and every incident that threatened delay ate into his ulcer. One day he envisaged his fellow star Laurence Harvey being off the picture for several days when a cannon wheel rolled over Harvey's foot. Fortunately, no bones were broken but his foot was swelling.

"Get him the hell to hospital," ordered Wayne, wondering how long Harvey would be incapacitated.

But Harvey refused to go. He ordered a bucket of boiling water and a bucket of ice. When these arrived, he dipped his foot first into the hot bucket and then the ice bucket, and kept repeating

(Opposite top) The troops of Santa Anna storm the Alamo's walls, while (bottom) cannon fire penetrates inside the mission-turned-fortress. (Right) John Wayne directed and produced his momentous contribution to the Epic; The Alamo in which he also starred as Davy Crockett. (Below) Captain William Travis (Laurence Harvey) dies fighting. (The Alamo – United Artists)

the process. "The hot and cold treatment," he calmly explained.

The following day he was back on the set.

Wayne's troubles were added to when a girl with a walk-on part was found murdered. She was 27-year-old La Lean Ethridge who at the beginning of production was just an extra. The Duke was impressed with her brief performance and promoted her to a featured role. She was told to leave her living quarters in nearby Spofford and move into Bracketville. While she packed her things Chester Harvey Smith, an extra who was in love with her, tried to prevent her going and stabbed her with, ironically enough, a Bowie knife.

Smith was arrested and five days later a trial was held. Fred Semaan, Smith's defender, served a subpoena on Wayne to appear as a witness. By now the Duke's troubles had snowballed and the budget had risen drastically. He had to borrow money from banks and friends, and put everything he

(Above) The Alamo is filled with the victorious Mexican troops of dictator Santa Anna. (Right) Mrs Dickinson (Joan O'Brien) her daughter Lisa (Aissa Wayne) and Travis's servant are the only survivors. (The Alamo – United Artists)

owned into the picture to reach the final figure of twelve million.

Semaan hadn't a hope of saving Smith who pleaded guilty, but he hoped to prove that Wayne's company was putting pressure on the D.A. to push the case harder than was necessary by getting Wayne to admit that a lot of scenes would need reshooting.

Served with the subpoena, Wayne called Semaan and said he wasn't coming.

"By God, if you don't, I'll have you thrown in jail," threatened the lawyer.

Reluctantly, wanting to press on with his twelve million dollar headache, Wayne took time off to turn up as a witness. He showed his disapproval on the witness stand and this only got Semaan madder than he already was with the Duke.

"Tell me, Mr. Payne . . . ." began Semaan, purposely intimidating Wayne. (There was another popular actor at that time called John Payne.)

"It's *Wayne*," bawled the star.

(Above) Bereavement for Eve (Carrol Baker)
and her sister Lillith (Debbie Reynolds).
Mountain man Linus (James Stewart) joins the family by marrying Eve. (Right)
John Ford directed Carroll Baker and George
Peppard in the Civil War episode of How
The West Was Won – (MGM Cinerama).

"I beg your pardon, Mr. Wayne," said Semaan, and after a few minutes added, "Now Mr. ah . . . is it Wayne or Payne?"

After the hearing, outside the courthouse, Wayne strode over to Semaan and the lawyer prepared for a broadside. Instead, Wayne grinned and said, "You kinda poured into me in there."

"Well, you asked for it," said Semaan.

"Yeah, I guess I did," beamed the Duke, and they shook hands.

Back on the set John Ford was on hand, and when viewing the rushes he said, "It's timeless. It's the greatest picture I've ever seen."

Sadly, The Alamo was a financial disaster for Wayne, but not for United Artists who made their money back on it. Wayne, unfortunately, had made some bad business deals in his need for extra financing, and he never recouped it. Artistically, despite what the critics say, it was a great success and was nominated for several Oscars.

Regardless of Wayne's Oscar-winning True Grit, The Alamo remains his finest achievement and long after his death it will stand as a monument to this great star.

Wayne was among a horde of stars in the giant Cinerama western How The West Was Won yet oddly enough had

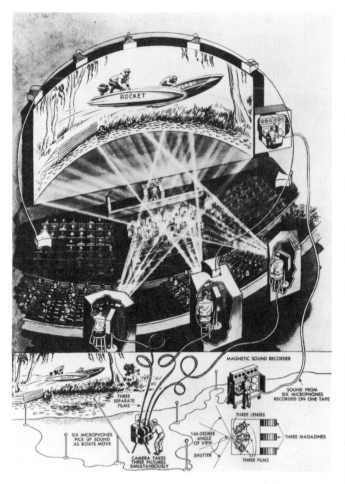

ROCKET FLASH

MAGNETIC SOUND RECORDER

SOUND FROM
SIX MICROPHONES
RECORDED ON ONE TAPE

THREE
SEPARATE
FILMS

SIX MICROPHONES
PICK UP SOUND
AS BOATS MOVE

146-DEGREE
ANGLE
OF VIEW

THREE LENSES

THREE MAGAZINES

THREE FILMS

SHUTTER

CAMERA TAKES
THREE PICTURES
SIMULTANEOUSLY

(*Above left*) *How cinerama achieved its effect.* (*Above right*) *Internal conflict between the railroad (Richard Widmark) and the army (George Peppard).* (*Right*) *Pioneering sisters Eve and Lillith.* (*Opposite*) *The heart-stopping train wreck were typical of Cinerama action sequences.* (How The West Was Won – *MGM Cinerama*).

only one major scene as General Sherman in the civil war sequence which John Ford directed. Many feel that this was the best of the five episodes in the film, the others being the journey West of a pioneering family, the gold rush, the railroads and the outlaws. To accommodate the complicated make-up of the picture, three directors worked in unison; Ford, as already mentioned, George Marshall, who directed the railroads, and Henry Hathway who directed the majority of the film and to whom, really, all the credit should go, according to James Stewart who also starred.

"Henry was pretty much responsible for the picture," he told me. "It took quite a while to do and there were problems storywise because of the different people directing it which sort of disconnected it. Henry talked the powers-that-be (MGM and Cinerama) into letting him fill in the gaps

that gave a better story line. He sort of took it upon himself and saved the film actually."

Bernard Smith produced this giant of a horse-opera which was the first story ever filmed in the old system of Cinerama which then required a camera which was really three cameras in one through which three films ran. For the giant curved screen presentation three projectors were needed to encompass a field of 145 degrees to create that you-are-there feeling. As money began to run out it became necessary to take certain stock shots from other films and, by trickery-pokery they cut the films into three strips to be compatible with the original Cinerama footage. These included a shot of Santa Anna's army on the march from *The Alamo*, and the famous civil war battle was in fact from MGM's *Raintree County*. The modern day scene at the end of the film was the ending to the first Cinerama film, *This Is Cinerama*.

Also in the cast were Karl Malden, George Peppard, Robert Preston, Carolyn Jones, Debbie Reynolds, Lee J.

Cobb, Richard Widmark and Carroll Baker.

In an interview with Carroll, I asked her if acting before the huge three lens camera proved a problem at all.

She said, "It was very difficult to adjust to that camera because it covered such a large area and tended to look around the corner for the curved effect. When you walked off a set with an ordinary camera you just walked straight off, but with this one you would often mess up a 'take' because you'd walk off and still be in shot, and you'd maybe make faces at the make-up girl and they'd shout, '*Hey, just a minute!*'

"There'd be no place to put the microphone because the camera photographed more of the sky than a normal camera, and you obviously couldn't put it to the side and you couldn't put it below you because the camera took in a lot more below your head as well as above. So often the mike would end up under porch steps or in a bush."

Although Carroll featured mainly in the first sequence with the family, she

did appear later at the opening of the civil war episode, directed by John Ford, which led eventually to her being cast in Ford's last great western, *Cheyenne Autumn*. Her memories of Ford are full of warmth and nostalgia.

"He was a great man and I feel very privileged to have worked with him. The wonderful thing about him was, not only was he a great director, but you became a part of his 'family' because when he went on location for months he used to gather all the actors around him and everybody ate dinner with him at night. Everybody would then be called upon to entertain. You had to play the guitar or dance or sing, and it was really like an old homestead dinner everynight. You *had* to be around pappy."

While *How The West Was Won* was before the cameras over many parts of America, almost simultaneously MGM and Cinerama were collaborating on another project, *The Wonderful World Of The Brothers Grimm*, the story of Hans Christian Andersson. It was the second and last Cinerama film with a

story to be filmed in the old system. By 1962 a single lens system had been perfected which was basically 70 mm film with the images squeezed slightly at the edges which spread out automatically when projected on a curved screen. Eventually, this squeezing at the edges was dropped and all further Cinerama pictures were shot simply in 70 mm. Although still projected on a giant curved screen, a Cinerama film was only really such in theory, depending on how it had been filmed. So directors filled their spectacular films with runaway wagons, speeding trains and swooping aeroplanes, always positioning the camera on whatever vehicle was used.

(*Right*) *Lillith finds herself torn between two men (*Gregory Peck *and* Robert Preston*) while Agatha (*Thelmer Ritter*) is looking for any* man. (*Below*) *The aftermath of the buffalo stampede leaves little impression on cold-hearted Mike King (*Richard Widmark*).* (How The West Was Won – *MGM Cinerama*)

That was Cinerama

One of Robert Shaw's 60 charges he performed as Custer Of The West (Cinerama—ABC)

Westerns continued to be a popular form of Cinerama entertainment and *Custer Of The West*, though not totally authentic in its portrayal of the glory-hunting General as played by Robert Shaw, had lots of Cinerama effects that made it such an enthralling experience.

It even introduced a new 'runaway' type sequence when a Sergeant escapes an Indian massacre by leaping onto a logging chute, grabs a passing log and rides down to the river with it. This sequence took three weeks to film, most of the time being spent building and testing boats to carry the camera. Two

were actually lost when they plunged into the foaming river. Stunt man Robert Hall, who played the Sergeant, made five trips down the chute with the log at speeds of around 40 miles an hour. Fifteen trips were taken by the cameramen.

There were also plenty of cavalry charges that the audience almost participated in. Robert Shaw led a total of 60 charges during the filming in Spain, more than Custer himself ever made. Shaw had never ridden before and he had to study riding for three weeks before filming started.

Producer Carl Foreman and director J. Lee Thompson, the team who made *The Guns Of Navarone*, got together again for *MacKenna's Gold*, a western starring Gregory Peck and Omar Sharif which was specifically filmed for the Cinerama screen. J. Lee Thompson gracefully accepts the derogatory view of most critics that the film has an uneasy pace. This, according to Thompson, is because the film was purposely set out and filmed by him for the Cinerama screen. However, someway through production Carl Foreman had a set-to with Cinerama and cancelled

151

(*Top*) Husband and wife Robert Shaw and Mary Ure played Mr and Mrs Custer. (*Centre*) Custer finds himself fighting alone at Little Big Horn. (*Bottom*) The Cheyennes secure Custer's place in history. (Custer Of The West – *Cinerama-ABC*)

their agreement. Thompson told Foreman that the film would not be a success on a flat screen but the producer wouldn't listen and that's why you never saw what would have been a most effective Cinerama experience on the giant screen.

The two most impressive of all the single-lensed Cinerama epics were undoubtedly the MGM productions *Grand Prix* and *2001; A Space Odyssey*.

For *Grand Prix*, director John Frankenheimer had remote control cameras attached to the racing cars so that the audience would be literally swept around the circuits. The stars of the film, like James Garner and Yves Montand, actually drove their cars and thirty two professional drivers made up the numbers.

Ask Frankenheimer today, 14 years after the film was made, if it was dangerous and he breaks out in a cold sweat.

"It was horrendous," he says. "It was a miracle that not one of those drivers were killed that year. If just one driver had been killed that would have been the end of the film. The following year six of them were killed. One of them was Lorenzo Bandini who was killed at Monte Carlo right at the same spot he had helped me to stage an accident. That was for the scene in which James Garner's car went into the water. We used the Monte Carlo rescue team for that. I told them we were going to throw Jimmy Garner into the water and I said, '*You guys get him out as fast as you can.*' '*We are ze best in ze world,*' they told me."

Frankenheimer went to Garner and said, "How do you feel about it?"

"It's colder 'n hell in that water," replied Garner.

"But do you want to do it?"

"Sure, but do you really think they'll get me out?" Garner asked.

"Absolutely," the director assured him. "They'll get you out for sure."

So in went Garner. "Roll the cameras," shouted Frankenheimer. "In you go," he told the rescue team.

"Now those cameras hold eight minutes of film," explains Frankenheimer. "We ran out of film before they even got to him. Garner almost drowned and then they almost ran over him with the rescue boat.

"One year later Bandini crashed at the same spot but he didn't go into the water. By the time the rescue team got

(*Above*) *James Garner's on-screen rescue turned into a nightmare for the actor when* (*Right*) *the Monte Carlo rescue team nearly failed to get to him quick enough.* (Grand Prix — MGM)

to him his car was in flames and he burned to death. They *should* have got him out, but nothing worked. The fire extinguishers weren't loaded. If that had happened during filming on the first race the film would have been over. Of course, I didn't tell Metro-Goldwyn-Mayer that. How they ever let the film be made, I'll never know. Out of the thirty two drivers I used, twenty one are now dead. The fact that nobody got hurt on that movie is a miracle."

2001: A Space Odyssey in Cinerama really proved to be "the ultimate trip." But what went on behind the scenes will probably remain one of life's greatest mysteries. An ex-member of the MGM publicity department told me that when he visited Borehamwood Studios where it was being filmed there the most he saw was a couple of space

suits hanging up. Nobody went on the set by orders of the producer/director Stanley Kubrick who was no doubt determined that nobody, not even Kirk Douglas, would tell him what to do this time.

The film's special effects created by Wally Veevers, Douglas Trumball, Con Pederson and Tom Howard were the real stars of the movie. You almost forget that any actors appeared in the picture. The three major roles were taken by Keir Dullea and Gary Lockwood as the astronauts Bowman and Poole, and Douglas Rain who virtually stole the acting honours as Hal 9000, the computer.

Keir Dullea confessed to me that at the time the film was made he had no indication as to what kind of film Kubrick was making.

"I spent about five months on the film," he told me, "We had a very slim script (written by Kubrick and Arthur C. Clarke) and I had no idea of the implications or the magnitude of the film or the effect it would have on people. I knew the mundane story of what the astronauts were doing, but I had no idea of the possible philosophies people could evolve from the film, and Kubrick never discussed the ultimate philosophy.

"I was playing an astronaut who had strange things happening to him, and just as the character didn't know what was happening to him, I didn't know either!"

Today, despite the boom in science fiction with box office success like *Star Wars* and *Alien, 2001: A Space Odyssey* stands as the only real epic about the vast void beyond our atmosphere and by far the best sci-fi movie of all time.

Other Cinerama movies that fared well were *The Magnificent Showman* which starred John Wayne as a circus owner and was Samuel Bronston's last film, *Battle Of The Bulge*, a giant war movie, *Krakatoa, East Of Java*, the last picture filmed specifically for Cinerama, and another western, *The Hallelujah Trail*, one of several in a sudden spate of epic-sized comedies that hit the movie market during the Sixties.

Believe it or not, *The Hallelujah Trail* was based on fact and is, besides being a large-scale comedy, something (with a little stretch of the imagination) of an historical movie. Producer/director John Sturges wasn't too bothered though about presenting facts. He wanted laughs. Oddly enough, at the time it didn't get many. The humour was very subtle for a comedy western; not at all knockabout like *Cat Ballou*. Yet in its own way, *The Hallelujah Trail* is very dry and very, very funny.

Burt Lancaster starred as a whiskey-drinking Colonel with orders to protect a wagon train of booze on route to Denver from hostile Indians, led by Martin Landau as Chief Walks-Stooped-Over (the only blue-eyed Indian ever), and the temperance marchers led by Lee Remick as Cora ("Women can remake the world") Massingale. However, the Denver Militia are uncertain

"Pie in the face can look funny on the screen but …!"

(Opposite top) Keir Dullea as astronaut Bowman in 2001:A Space Odyssey *(MGM)*

(Opposite bottom) The epic mood of The Hallelujah Trail *is captured in this still. (Right) Stars Jim Hutton and Burt Lancaster with director John Sturges in between scenes of* The Hallelujah Trail. *(Below left) Colonel Gearhart, the morning after the night before, demands peace and quiet. (Below right) John Sturges supervises Burt Lancaster's hangover* (The Hallelujah Trail – *United Artists*).

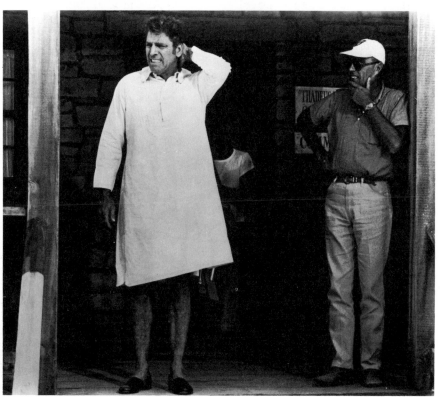

(*Right*) *Louise (Pamela Tiffin) gives daddy that little girl look.* (*Bottom*) *The US cavalry goes into action. Its mission: get them females the hell out of that fort!* (The Hallelujah Trail – *United Artists*)

of the cavalry's power to stop these two parties and they come out to meet the train with Orcale ("Thar now, I see it!") Jones (Donald Pleasence), who sees all, leading them straight into a sandstorm and losing his followers. In the middle of this confusion is Frank ("Damn it, I'm a good Republican") Wallingham, the owner of the wagon train, played by the biggest scene stealer of them all, Brian Keith. Also helping to provide the laughs were Jim Hutton as a Captain in the Colonel's command and Pamela Tiffin as the Colonel's daughter in love with the Captain in the Colonel's command and star pupil of Miss Massingale.

The movie was filmed in the summer of 1964 in Gallup, New Mexico where the weather is supposed to be hot and dry. Not in 1964! That year saw rain, hail, thunder, flash floods, hell and high water. Apparently the local Indians had been praying for rain to bring an

(*Above*) *Ethel Merman in fine voice – yelling, not singing!* (*Top right and right*) *Edie Adams and Sid Caesar generally having a mad time.* (It's A Mad, Mad, Mad, Mad World – *United Artists*).

end to a drought, and they didn't know how to stop it! Which was unfortunate because they wanted very much to be film stars for Mr. Sturges.

The Hallelujah Trail is notable, if for nothing else, for introducing the Western genre's nastiest heavie, Donald Pleasence, a noted and respected actor of the British theatre. This being his first western produced two snags; he couldn't ride and he wasn't particularly adept at producing an American accent. Still, he had to learn both.

"We were shooting a scene where I'm leading the Denver Militia and trying to sound like an American," Donald Pleasence told me, "and I said, '*C'mon! Keep right b'hand me.*' There was a little boy who'd been watching and he said to me, '*Hey, mister, are you supposed to be talking American?*'"

Still on the Cinerama trail, Stanley Kramer's *It's A Mad, Mad, Mad, Mad, World* is one of the biggest and funniest comedies of all time.

It all started when a letter arrived on Stanley Kramer's desk from screenwriter William Rose. He had an idea for a story which centred on a chase. It simply revolved around a group of very ordinary people who learn of the location of £125,000. After studying the ten thousand word story, Kramer sent for William Rose to discuss the project further.

"When Mr. Kramer and I met," says Rose, "he asked me to tell him briefly how I proposed to end the story. I talked, for perhaps ten minutes, explaining the final half of the picture. At the end of that time he stood up, extended his hand and said, '*You have a deal*.' I turned to my agent and he said, '*Shake the man's hand*.' And that was the beginning."

Rose returned to England to work on his script which turned into a 20 month task. In August, 1961, he flew back to Hollywood with his 320 page script called *Something A Little Less Serious*. Kramer loved the script but suggested the film be called *One Damn Thing After Another*. Then he changed his mind and thought of *It's A Mad World*. Rose suggested two *Mads* and then

Kramer doubled him, arriving at the final title.

The first actor to be signed was Spencer Tracy, one of Kramer's favourites, and the others soon followed; Milton Berle, Dorothy Provine, Ethel Merman, Dick Shawn, Sid Caesar, Buddy Hackett, Mickey Rooney, Phil Silvers, Jimmy Durante, Terry-Thomas, Eddie "Rochester" Anderson and Peter Falk.

One of the most important aspects of the film was the special effects, created by Danny Lee and his department. They had to explode 6,000 fireworks around Sid Caesar and Edie Adams in a hardware cellar; build a garage that comes apart when big

Jonathan Winters tears it to pieces; design a fire engine that would throw actors one by one from the top of its 100 foot ladder, and many other spectacular stunts.

Lee's proudest achievement was the contraption they built to run Durante's car off a cliff. It was radio controlled and put together with bits of electronic equipment which they acquired from the laboratories of the California Institute of Technology and nearby aerospace plants. Danny controlled the car from a mile away, starting the vehicle and steering it at a speed of 80 miles an hour and sending it over a cliff.

Some of the *It's A Mad, Mad, Mad, Mad World* performers turned up again in what for me is *the* great comedy epic, *The Great Race*, directed in 1965 by Blake Edwards. They were Peter Falk, Dorothy Provine and Danny Lee. While both Peter and Dorothy stole every scene they were in, the film's principals

(*Above right*) *The Great Leslie* (*Tony Curtis*) *puts Miss DuBois in a fix.* (*Below*) *They're off!* (The Great Race — Warner Bros)

(Top left) Hezekiah (Kennan Wynn) gets a pie in the eye. Leslie doesn't. (Top right) "Rum – I never mix my pies." (Above) Miss DuBois gets it in the mush! (Above right) Leslie finally gets his just desert. (The Great Race – Warner Bros)

were Jack Lemmon, Tony Curtis and Natalie Wood. Set in the early Nineteen-hundreds, it tells of a race around the world with protagonists Professor Fate (Lemmon), a black hearted villain clad in a suit, the colour of which matched his heart; The Great Leslie (Curtis), described by Fate as whose "hair is always tidy and your suit is always white and your car is always clean. You I hate." Then there is pretty,

feminine but feminist Maggie DuBois (Natalie Wood), whose clothes are generally as pink as her complexion.

Also starring were Leslie's and Fate's cars. They were specially built by Warner Bros, craftsmen and designed by art director Fernando Carrere and special effects wizard Danny Lee. A number of duplicates of these cars were made for use in the film and all were insured for 200,000 dollars.

Looking like 200,000 dollars was Natalie Wood, probably America's finest all-round actress when it comes to comedy, high drama and soap opera. For her role in *The Great Race* she had to use swords in a duel with Tony Curtis and ride side saddle (but not at the same time). Never having done

either before she was trained in the art of fencing by former US champion and Olympic coach Josef Vince. To learn to ride sidesaddle she went twice a week to a San Fernando Valley ranch to practise keeping her undeniably nice seat with both feet on the same side of the horse.

The highlight of the film is the celebrated pie throwing sequence. This took eight very messy days to shoot during which an estimated 2,357 pies were thrown, bowled, pushed into faces and generally littered around. About 75 pies landed on Jack Lemmon, but then at this point in the film he was playing a duel role and getting twice as many pies in an episode which was a spoof on *The Prisoner Of Zenda*.

(Above) Prof. Fate (Jack Lemmon) and Max (Peter Falk) fail again. (Left) Prof. Fate's version of "The Prisoner of Zenda." (The Great Race – Warner Bros.)

(Opposite top) Cool, calm reporter Maggie DuBois gets à hot story out West. (Opposite Bottom) Leslie has a hold on Miss DuBois. (The Great Race – Warner Bros).

Says Lemmon, "Pie in the face may look funny, but a little goes a long way, and after a while your eyes begin to burn, and the pie filling stiffens up and the sock begins to feel more like a dish of marbles than a chocolate mousse!"

On the last day's shooting of this scene Blake Edwards finally called "Cut" for the last time, believing he would never see another pie being thrown again. Suddenly 200 pies, which the cast and crew had held back unbeknown to Edwards, came flying at him from all directions. Blake Edwards ended up with more pie on his face (and all over him for that matter) than anybody else in the film.

Although *The Great Race* had people almost rolling in the aisles (at least, it did at the various screenings of the film I attended), the critics panned it. Surprisingly, the most popular of all the comedy epics is *Those Magnificent Men In Their Flying Machines* (1965) which, I'm afraid, didn't make a great impression on me. Still, it made a mint at the box-office and boasted a cast of international actors and comedians including Sarah Miles, Stuart Whitman, James Fox, Robert Morley, Gert Frobe, Eric Sykes, Terry Thomas, Red Skelton, Benny Hill, Flora Robson and Tony Hancock.

Ken Annakin, had long wanted to make a serious film about the early days of flying. Then he discovered that writer Jack Davies, with whom he had collaborated on *The Fast Lady, Crooks Anonymous* and *A Very Important Person*, was developing an original screenplay treatment about the same subject but in a comedy vein. And so *Those Magnificent Men* was launched.

"The collaboration with Jack Davies on *Flying Machines* was probably at its very best," Annakin told me, "because he used to live with me and my family, and whenever we saw an opportunity to develop the script we took it. For instance, there's a scene where Gert Frobe gets into his 'plane, and this character has never flown before; he takes the guide book and looks at it and says, 'No. 1. Sit down,' and that was simply devised on the spot."

Much, much funnier was the follow-up, *Monte Carlo Or Bust* (called in America *Those Daring Young Men In Their Jaunty Jollopies*).

It was the same formula as *Flying Machines* but on the ground. In fact, it was not unlike *The Great Race* and even had Tony Curtis as the hero, only he was just a little wet behind the ears in this one, unlike the Great Leslie. There was also Susan Hampshire, Terry-Thomas, Eric Sykes, Gert Frobe, Peter Cook and Dudley Moore.

Again it was directed by Ken Annakin who collaborated on the screen-

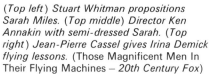

(Top left) Stuart Whitman propositions Sarah Miles. (Top middle) Director Ken Annakin with semi-dressed Sarah. (Top right) Jean-Pierre Cassel gives Irina Demick flying lessons. (Those Magnificent Men In Their Flying Machines – 20th Century Fox)

(Right) Chester (Tony Curtis) reveals his plans to race to Monte Carlo to scheming Sir Cuthbert (Terry Thomas) and his butler Perkins (Eric Sykes). (Bottom) When their car flies over a cliff edge, Major Dawlish (Peter Cook) coolly remarks to Lt. Kt Barrington (Dudley Moore) "Land There!" (Monte Carlo Or Bust – Paramount)

play with Jack Davies. It wasn't intended as a follow up to *Flying Machines*. In fact Annakin got the idea to do the famous car rally some years before the aerobatic comedy took off. It was while Annakin was filming *The Seekers* in Australia that he met rally driver Ken Warton who related tales of car rallies and some of the incredible things that happened. That was the seed of *Monte Carlo Or Bust*. Because of the success of *Flying Machines* Annakin looked for something in the same genre and so he put *Monte Carlo* on the road.

"Jack and I had already made one film about cars – *The Fast Lady*," says Annakin. "While working on that we had built together a good team of stunt drivers. So we sent a driver to the next Monte Carlo Rally for experience.

"Later we went into rallying with more depth and got a team to do six months' research on the subject. They came up with a vast amount of true stories of incidents that had happened to the drivers.

"One year, some competitors cheated by using a repair truck on the rally. The next year a furniture van teetered around Europe with cars in it. If the

(Above) Ken Annakin with Tony Curtis.
(Above right) Betty (Susan Hampshire)
holds on tight when the car she is in hangs
precariously over a cliff while (Right)
Chester hangs on even tighter. (Monte
Carlo Or Bust – Paramount)

crooked driver messed up one car he simply waited for the furniture van and got into the other car. We used this last idea in the film for Terry-Thomas.

"Another real incident was used in the scene when Tony Curtis arrives late at the Dover Ferry. The ferry is some 12 feet away from the quayside, so Curtis revs up the car and charges across the gap, making a jump of some 17 feet. That really happened to some rally driver.

"A stunt driver did the jump. We had everything prepared with elastic and sandbags, but the car made it. It stove in the entire front, but it didn't matter as we were able to switch to the second model of the same car."

Another perilous stunt had Tony Curtis' car see-sawing precariously on a frozen waterfall. The stuntmen did this for real on an actual waterfall and then back in the studios Tony Curtis and Susan Hampshire, as his passenger, went through the scene. It was still pretty dangerous for Tony who had to dangle from the car some eighteen feet off the ground. Fortunately, Tony was (and still is) a very fit man and more than used to this kind of moviemaking.

Sadly, Monte Carlo Or Bust wasn't as big a hit as its predecessor, which it deserved to be. It didn't harm Annakin's reputation though. He was becoming increasingly associated with big scale films and during the Sixties he worked on the two biggest war movies of that decade, The Longest Day and The Battle Of The Bulge.

"We never had it that rough on D. Day."

"When Zanuck asked me to do *The Longest Day*," Annakin said, "I'd never done a really big war picture before. I'd done the *Planter's Wife* years before, but never anything really big."

On *The Longest Day* (1962) Annakin got to film the British forces landing on the Normandy Beaches. Like *How The West Was Won*, this had a number of directors. Andrew Marton, who is actually a first rate Second Unit Director, directed the American battle scenes and Bernhard Wicki did the German episodes. Then there was Darryl F. Zanuck, who produced the picture, putting in his own scenes but leaving all the coordination and filling in to Elmo Williams. Happily, Zanuck and Williams did a much better job of this, the most spectacular of all the war films, than they did of *Cleopatra*.

It's impossible to get all the cast in here and now, but you can toss around

(*Top*) Major Howard (Richard Todd) leads his men on the assault at the Orne River Bridge. (*Left*) Major Werner Pluskat (Hans Christian Blech) survives an attack on a German division. (*Bottom left*) John Wayne as Vandervoot. (*Below*) Irina Demick poses with a carbine in between shots of The Longest Day (*20th Century Fox.*)

(Top left) Michael Medwin was one of the British stars in The Longest Day. (Top right) Schultz (Richard Beymer) wins stacks of money in a crap game before the great invasion begins. (Left) "I just don't know how they did it," claims Tommy Sands while he, Robert Wagner and Paul Anka wait between scenes. (The Longest Day – 20th Century Fox)

names like John Wayne, Richard Burton, Peter Lawford, Robert Mitchum, Henry Fonda, Rod Steiger, Sean Connery, Richard Todd, Curt Jurgens, Gerd Froebe (Gert Frobe), Red Buttons, Jeffrey Hunter and dozens upon dozens of others.

Wherever possible, Zanuck filmed at the original settings on and around the Normandy beaches. Many of the people depicted in the film were still alive and visited the set to meet the actors portraying them. Janine Boitard, a French Resistance worker who saved 68 Allied fliers from the Germans, often met with her film counterpart, newcomer Irina Demich and commented, "I wish I'd been as pretty as that!"

Robert Ryan portrayed General James Gavin who, when Ryan was filming at Studio Boulogne, went along and gave the actor some added information and told how when he and his men parachuted into France on 'D' Day, he was wearing his West Point ring. Listening to this conversation was John Wayne. He pointed out his own ring and the General agreed it was very similar to the one he had worn. Wayne then loaned the ring to Ryan who played his scenes wearing it.

Lord Lovat, who led his men ashore at Sword Beach and saw action at the Orne River Bridge, came to the loc-

ation to see Peter Lawford doing the same some two decades later. Lovat watched as Lawford was supposed to have leapt off a landing craft and land knee deep in the icy Atlantic. Lawford was equipped with special, watertight nylon underwear to keep him dry. The wardrobe lady had told him not to zip the garment to the top, telling him he wouldn't need it that high.

But when he jumped into the sea it wasn't knee-deep. It was 6 feet deep and his garment rapidly filled up with water, dragging him down. With a great deal of effort plus the desire to live to spend the money Zanuck was paying him, he hauled himself ashore.

Said Lord Lovat, "We never had it *that* rough on 'D' Day!"

The landing of 225 American Rangers at Pointe-du-Hoc and their daring scaling of 100-foot cliffs while under heavy gunfire was filmed where it happened. The Rangers' mission was to dispose of German guns concealed in bunkers.

Among the actors involved in this scene were Robert Wagner, Tommy Sands, Fabian, and Paul Anka. Cornelius Ryan, who wrote the book on which the film was based, also visited the set.

"This is the spot all right," he said grimly. "It was a brutal episode; a sacrifice of American lives and nothing

(*Above*) "*The puniness of men against these great looming tanks.*" (*Right*) *Conrad* (*Hans Christian Blech*) *escapes the inferno.* (The Battle Of The Bulge – *Warner Bros*)

was accomplished. When the Rangers got in here, they found no guns. There weren't any. The Germans had never installed them."

Tommy Sands gazed up at the jagged rocks a hundred feet above him.

"I just don't know how they did it," he said. "Just to climb those rocks takes a lot of guts. But to do it with someone shooting at you as well . . . ."

While, for most people, it was a pretty miserable experience, one man who did enjoy playing at war games in a really big way was Ken Annakin. He told me, "I rather got to like it on *The Longest Day*. Then I got the chance to do *Battle Of The Bulge* which was more fun than ever with 82 tanks."

Battle Of The Bulge is probably the best film Annakin has yet made. It again belongs to that group of spectacles shot for the Cinerama screen, a factor that was in part the attraction for Annakin.

"I'd never shot in Cinerama before.

166

(*Top*) *Filming an action sequence and* (*Centre*) *the results on film.* (*Bottom*) *Lt. Col. Kiley* (*Henry Fonda*) *and Wolemski* (*Charles Bronson*) *move the men up.* (The Battle Of The Bulge — *Warner Bros*)

I wanted to show the puniness of human beings against these great looming tanks which come like monsters out of the earth, and that despite the great advantage of the machines, the bravery of men can still come through. That was my theme, because the picture didn't have a theme when it was first started.''

It was yet another star-laden cast; Henry Fonda, Robert Shaw, Robert Ryan (who was always in the best war movies), Dana Andrews, George Montgomery, Ty Hardin, Pier Angeli, Barbara Werle, Charles Bronson and Telly Savalas.

As though taking over where Samuel Bronston left off, Philip Yordon took to producing films and made this spectacle in collaboration with Milton Sperling. Like the man who taught him how to shoot an epic, Yordon made his base in Spain and filmed *Battle Of The Bulge* in the frozen wastes of the Nevacerrada.

Three Ultra-Panavision/Cinerama cameras under the supervision of Jack Hildyard soaked up the stark locations and took in the sweep of four thousand extras in German uniforms and two thousand in American uniforms, many of them fighting it out in nearly one hundred authentic Tiger tanks and almost just as many Shermans.

The film that lifted the war movie out of its own genre and into that of the epic is *The Guns Of Navarone.* Primarily produced by Carl Foreman with a little help from Cecil Ford, and directed by J. Lee Thompson, it was filmed on the exotic Greek Island of Rhodes in the Aegean sea. Unfortunately, it was not an island ideally suited to cater to the making of a large motion picture. Carl Foreman was able to resolve the problems after a series of personal conferences with His Excellency the Prime Minister of Greece, Constantine Karamanlis. This led to governmental co-operation such as the loaning to the film company of six Royal Hellenic Navy destroyers, several air-sea rescue boats, numerous helicopters, tanks and all the military hardware needed for the film.

On February 15th, 1960, the whole film unit invaded Rhodes. Carl Foreman all but took over the Hotel Miramare, which was still under construction, to house his director, his actors Gregory Peck, David Niven, Anthony Quinn, Stanley Baker, Anthony Quale, James Darren, Gia Scala

(*Above*) *The battle rages on.* (The Battle Of The Bulge — *Warner Bros*). (*Right*) *Pappadimos* (*Anthony Quinn*) *and Mallory* (*Gregory Peck*) *administer to the severely wounded Andrea* (*Anthony Quale*). (The Guns of Navarone — *Columbia*)

and Irene Papas, plus the whole film crew.

There were the usual, expected accidents such as cuts and bruises, especially when the stars were battered and half-drowned in 250,000 gallons of water at Shepperton Studios in England. They were filming shots of the scene in which their Greek fishing boat is smashed against the rocks of the island of Navarone. Water is often the most dangerous natural element to be used in films, as the extras in *Noah's Ark* discovered to their cost, but fortunately by 1960 control on such scenes had been tightened. Or should have been. The effects of 16 tons of water cascading out of six jet spouts from above was actually an unknown quantity and neither J. Lee Thompson nor the special effects people knew for certain how the actors would fare. They fared all right, but not without a few abrasions.

It's amazing that nobody was killed back in the Aegean when a too realistic explosion blew a hole in the hull of a

The Great Leslie (Tony Curtis) endears himself to Prince Devnick (Jack Lemmon). (The Great Race — Warner Bros).

Maggie Dubois (Natalie Wood) begins The Great Race. (Warner Bros).

Another great race, this one in Cinerama. James Garner in Grand Prix (*MGM*).

(*Opposite*) *Charlton Heston as General Gordon in* Khartoum (*United Artists*).

(*Below*) *On location with* The Battle of the Bulge. (*Warner Bros*).

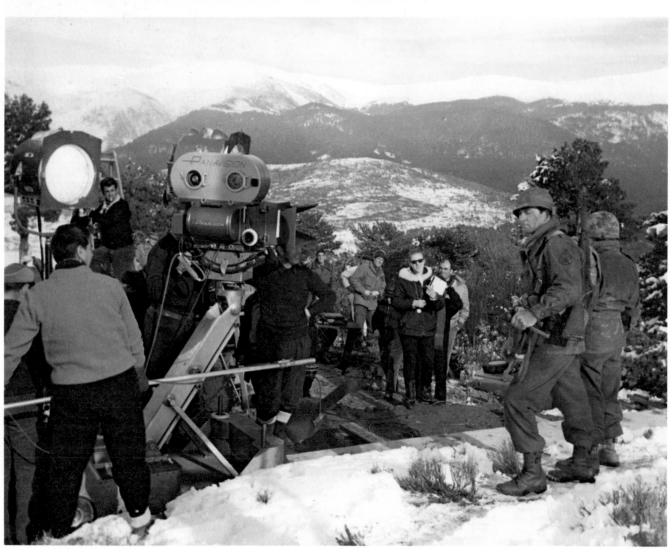

The ultimate trip in Cinerama. (2001: A
Space Odyssey — *MGM*).

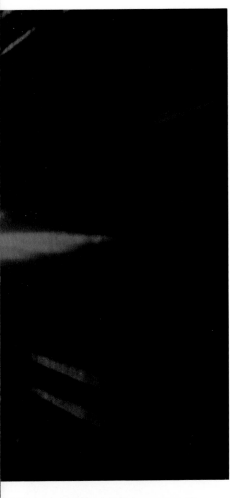

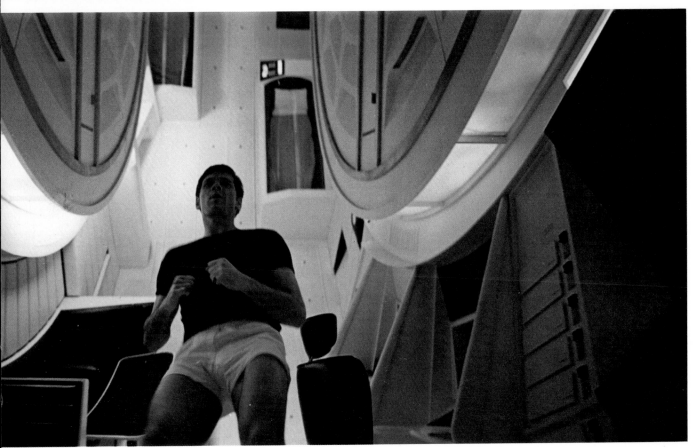

Keeping fit in outer space. (2001: A Space Odyssey – *MGM*).

As Messalina, *Brenda Lee had her fair share of admirers.*

Hercules holds his own in Hercules Unchained, *starring Steve Reeves.*

Ol' Herc with his leading lady, Sylvia Koskina. (Hercules Unchained)

(*Top*) *The latest version of the Crucifixion of Christ. This time with Brian Deacon in the title role of* Jesus. (*Right*) *The resurrected Christ.*

Greek patrol boat. Carl Foreman had to foot the cost to the Royal Hellenic Navy.

The Greek Royal Family came to watch the filming one day and invited Foreman, Thompson and the cast to a party aboard the destroyer they had travelled in from Athens.

The actual guns of Navarone were designed with the help of military experts in England, and constructed over a period of five months at a factory outside London and finally moved to Shepperton Studios.

Odly enough, *The Guns Of Navarone* is one of the very few really big movies made about the colourful country of Greece. It is a land steeped in ancient legends and heroes and it is surprising that, unlike the legends and history of ancient Rome, the Greek formula has been virtually ignored by film-makers.

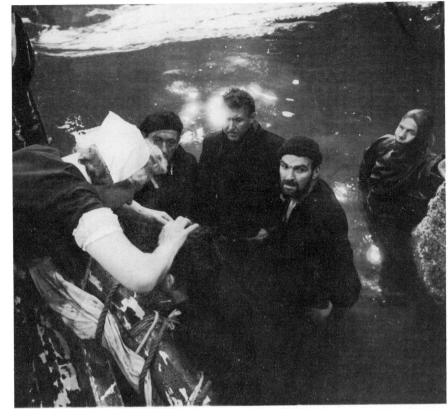

(*Top right*) *Gregory Peck has his head tended to after being injured in the studio tank.* (*Below*) *Maria* (*Irene Papas*) *kneels over the body of traitor Anna* (*Gia Scala*) *whom Mallory executed.* (The Guns Of Navarone — *Columbia*)

The face that launched a thousand spin-offs

The giant wooden horse is hauled into Troy. (Helen Of Troy — Warner Bros).

Of the few films about ancient Greece made and undoubtedly the best is the strangely underrated *Alexander The Great*, made in 1956. Richard Burton starred in the title role of the great Grecian hero and conqueror. Fredric March was King Philip of Macedonia, Danielle Darrieux played Alexander's mother, Olympus, and Claire Bloom was Barsine. Also in the cast was Peter Cushing who suffered much sickness while on location in Spain. Robert Rossen produced and directed, bringing to the screen not just a great spectacle, which it certainly was, but a powerful drama, giving Richard Burton the chance to prove his capabilities went far beyond the limited potential of his role in *The Robe*.

The only other big Grecian movies were *The 300 Spartans* starring Rich-ard Egan, and Robert Wise's *Helen Of Troy* which, was as exciting as Achilles with a crab at his heel. However, the battles were superb, which was only natural since they were staged by Yakima Canutt. It was filmed in Italy where director Raoul Walsh happened to find himself when *Helen Of Troy* went desperately over schedule. Walsh still had some time do for Warner Bros, the studio backing *Helena*, and so Walsh worked off his contract by shooting the battles with Canutt while Wise got on with the first unit. Unhappily, Robert Wise's contribution was not up to the more spectacular element of the picture, care of Canutt.

Obviously, the Italians later felt they could do the Helena story better and, during the Sixties when that country produced more epics than it did pizzas, they produced *The Trojan Horse* starring none other than the man of steel himself, Steve Reeves. In those early years of the sixties and the last couple of years of the fifties Steve Reeves made a fortune out of his heroic exploits in Italian cheapo epics. The thing about those films is, while they may not have given much to the world of art, they were great fun, although Reeves always took his work seriously.

He first came to the fore with *Hercules* which showman Joe Levine brought over to Britain and America and successfully sold. Then he did the same with the sequel *Hercules Unchained*.

Another muscle man from America who found fame in such films was Gordon Scott, who had effectively played Tarzan a few times. He and Steve Reeves came face to face in

Duel Of The Titans, which was directed by Sergio Corbucci, who later made some of the better Italian westerns. One of the collaborators on the screenplay was none other than Sergio Leone.

Corbucci directed Reeves again in *The Son Of Spartacus*, a sort of sequel to the Kirk Douglas epic, and while we're on sequels, Reeves played his *Trojan Horse* role again in *The Last Glory Of Troy*.

While Hercules, Goliath, Samson, Ursus and other muscle-bound heroes dominated the market, the women had their look-in in the shapely form of *Messalina*, starring Belinda Lee in the title role. Other adventures of the empress came along under such inane titles as *Messalina Against The Son Of Hercules*.

Like the Italian westerns later, these mini-epics provided income for a number of not so busy American actors like Victor Mature (*The Tartars* and *Hannibal*), Stewart Granger (*The Swordsman Of Siennea*) and Cameron Mitchell (*Last Of The Vikings* and *Caesar The Conqueror*).

(Left) Helen (Rossana Podesta) and Paris (Jack Sernas). (Below) Hector (Harry Andrews) with Helen and Paris. (Helen Of Troy — Warner Bros)

(*Above*) The 300 Spartans — *20th Century Fox*. (*Left*) *Richard Burton as* Alexander The Great — *United Artists*.

(*Opposite top left*) *During a break in filming of* Alexander The Great, *director Robert Rossen chats to Richard Burton.* (*Top right*) *Hercules (Steve Reeves) ripples for some Italian beauty in* Hercules Unchained. (*Bottom*) *Italian epics like* Hercules Unchained *may have been modestly budgeted, but they were nothing if not lavish.*

"The film industry doesn't like costume epics. The public like them, but not the industry."

Brian Deacon in the title role of *Jesus*.

Hercules and Goliath, Steve Reeves and Gordon Scott; they are all things of the past and we'll never see such films again. Thank the Lord for that, some might say. But the decline of these Italian epics marks the decline of the whole epic genre. The Italians only wanted a piece of the action, but what action is there left?

Well, all is not totally lost. In the past few years some films such as *The Wind And The Lion* and *The Message* have tried to evoke the splendour of the genre. But what of the Biblical epic and the films of ancient history? True, there was *Jesus Of Nazareth* and *Moses The Lawgiver*, but both were made as television series and even when seen in a theatre, gone are the Ultra-Panavision shaped images and the super-stereophonic sound and the

cinematic pace, because, as TV series, they last something like six or seven hours, and when cut down to two and a half hours or three hours, something of significance has to go.

So what's the good news? "The Genesis Project", that's the good news. Producer John Heyman has for the past six years been busily filming the Bible in Israel. Yes, the *whole* Bible! The thing is, it won't be completed until 1993 if all goes according to schedule.

So far in the can is the whole of Genesis, but only as twenty-minute episodes for showing in schools and churches. Realising that the whole project needed a commercial boost, Heyman set about filming the Gospel according to Luke as a feature film, and called it simply *Jesus*.

The claim is that *Jesus* is far closer

to the story of Jesus as written in the Bible than any other film. It is certainly a unique venture in that everyone, except the Israeli actors and technicians, involved in the production are Christians and their prime object is to bring the Gospel to the world in a commercial way.

The only English actor in the film is Brian Deacon who plays Christ. He spent seven months making the film under very uncomfortable conditions. He experienced the hostility felt between Arab and Jew as they filmed in Arab villages. Troops had to accompany the whole unit and one night Arabs attacked some of the unit's trucks and stole some equipment, but fortunately there were few other incidents of violence.

The only sets that had to be built

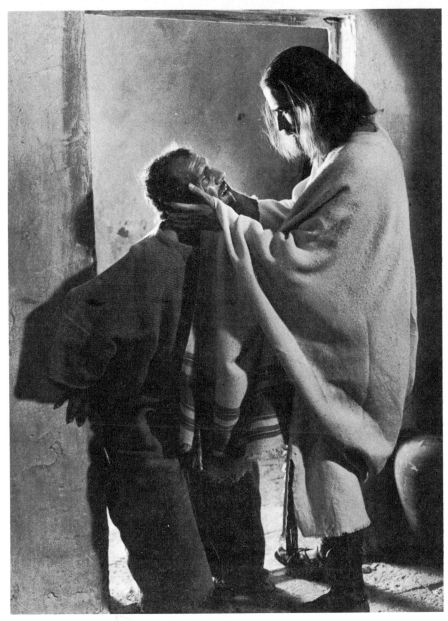

(*Left*) *Our Lord is nailed to the cross, while* (*below*) *He cures a man with dropsy in these scenes from* Jesus.

were the Temple and a synagogue, but otherwise everything in the film is real.

One of Brian's worst experiences was being crucified. He explained to me the method in which the Romans crucified people.

"They nailed you through your wrists and ankles, and they also put a peg under your crutch. There was no support for your feet, the point being that you suffocated. Everytime you let the weight down onto your ankles the pain would be terrific, so you· would have to lift yourself up again, and down again. Everytime you lifted your rib cage, you would be carrying the weight there, and you had to keep releasing the weight back onto your ankles. Eventually your rib cage would collapse and that was why on the Sabbath people on the cross had their legs broken so they could no longer haul themselves up. Jesus died quicker because he had suffered such a severe beating beforehand.

"So this is more or less how they put me and the other two (who played the thieves) on the crosses. The crosses were hauled up into place with ropes so we had no support for our feet. In between shots they'd run up with ladders as support for our feet. Within three minutes I'd lost all feeling in my arms and it was frightening. When the cross goes up it goes just beyond the perpendicular and you're certain you're going to go straight down again. We spent five very uncomfortable days doing that."

During the seven months Brian made himself ill because he supressed all his frustrations, feeling it would be wrong to release them and get angry while portraying Christ. He ended up with a severe stomach pain as though he had an ulcer.

Jesus promises to include many incidents recorded in the Bible that other film-makers have neglected. There are also some changes for the better. We actually see the resurrected Christ and instead of being solemn and serious, he is shown to be glad and happy. It was something that Brian felt unsure about at first. They were filming the scene when Jesus appears to his disciples, in a very smelly barn in which the air was so bad that many of the crew wore protective masks.

The director, Peter Sykes, prepared Brian for the scene and wanted it to be a happy moment. Brian first did it the way he thought it should be done which Sykes thought too serious.

"Look, I think you should have a big smile on your face," he told Brian. "You've done it your way and I think it is too stern. Let's do it my way with a big smile and a really warm, '*Peace be with you.*'"

Brian did it with a smile and, according to Brian, it is unique and perfect.

"When Jesus came back to them he wasn't sad," he told me. "I'm sure it was a moment of joy, and they all must have hit the roof."

Although Hayman intends to continue making his short films for non-theatrical showings, it now looks as though he will simultaneously shoot the stories as feature films as well with a hope of releasing one big picture a year until the whole of the Bible is on film. It should be something to look forward to.

Also to look forward to, if he can get the money, is Peter Snell's planned project, *1066*. Charlton Heston will play Alfred the Great and hopefully George C. Scott will portray William the Conqueror. According to Snell it will be "in the manner of *El Cid*", which can't be bad. The only problem is getting the money.

"The film industry doesn't like costume epics," Snell told me. "The public like them, but not the industry."

It's a subject Heston has been wanting to make for years, only he could never find the right script. This seems to be the one, because when I saw him in London in 1979 I asked him about Snell's project and he said, "I'd love to do it, if only he can get the backing."

As Snell says, it only needs someone to make a successful super-colossal costume spectacle and then everyone will make one. If only someone like Peter Snell can get the chance. Or maybe it will be John Heyman who lights the fuse. Only Heyman doesn't intend to stand back and retire. At least not until 1993.

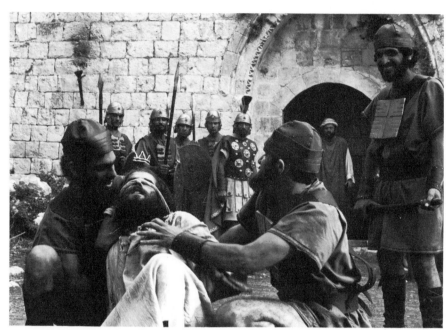

(*Right*) *Herod's soldiers mock Jesus and the final degradation (*below*) is to be crucified. Scenes from* Jesus.

The Great Epics

A personal selection of the outstanding epics, whether they be artistically superior or just plain entertaining. Names in italics indicate individual artistic merit to those who, in the author's humble opinion, provided something a little extra to their film's final value. For instance, without the music of Miklos Rozsa, *Sodom And Gommorah* would undoubtedly have lost much of its limited polish. But this is not to deny credit to other artists involved. Oscar winners are also listed.

THE ALAMO 1960 United Artists.

John Wayne (Col. Davey Crockett), Laurence Harvey (Col. Travis), *Richard Widmark* (Jim Bowie), Frankie Avalon (Smitty), Patrick Wayne (Capt Bonham), Linda Cristal (Flaca), Joan O'Brien (Mrs. Dickenson), Chill Wills (Beekeeper), Ken Curits (Capt. Dickinson), Aissa Wayne (Lisa), Richard Boone (Sam Houston). Producer/director; *John Wayne*. Screenplay; *James Edward Grant*. Director of photography; *William H. Clothier*. Music; *Dimitri Tiomkin*. Running time; 211 minutes.
Oscars (1) Best sound (Jack Solomon).
Nominations also include Best Film, Best Photography (Clothier), Best Music (Tiomkin), Best Supporting Actor (Wills), Best Song "The Green Leaves of Summer" (Tiomkin, Paul Francis Webster).

ALEXANDER THE GREAT 1956 United Artists

Richard Burton (Alexander), *Fredric March* (Philip), Danielle Darrieux (Olympias), Claire Bloom (Barsine), Harry Andrews (Darius), Barry Jones (Aristotle), Stanley Baker (Attalus), Niaall MacGinnis (Parmenio), Peter Cushing (Memo), Michael Horden (Demonsthenes), Peter Wyngarde (Pausanias).
Dir/prod; *Robert Rossen*. Photo; *Robert Krasker*. Mus; Mario Nascimbene. 165 minutes.

ANTONY AND CLEOPATRA 1972

Charlton Heston (Mark Antony), Hildegard Neil (Cleopatra), *Eric Porter* (Enobarbus), *John Castle* (Octavius), Fernando Rey (Lepidus), Juan Luis Galiardo (Alexas), Freddie Jones (Pompey).
Dir; *Charlton Heston*, Prod; Peter Snell, Scr; adapted by Charlton Heston, Photo; *Rafael Pacheco*, Mus; *John Scott*, 160 minutes.

AROUND THE WORLD IN EIGHTY DAYS United Artists 1956

David Niven (Phileas Fogg), Cantinflas (Passepartout), Shirley MacLaine (Princess Aouda), *Robert Newton* (Inspector Fix), with guest stars including Charles Boyer, John Carradine, Ronald Colman, Noel Coward, Finlay Currie, Marlene Dietrich, John Gielgud, Sir Cedric Hardwicke, Trevor Howard, Glynis Johns, Buster Keaton, Beatrice Lillie, Peter Lorre, Victor McLaglen, John Mills, George Raft, Frank Sinatra.
Dir; Michael Anderson, Prod; *Mike Todd*, Scr; James Poe, John Farrow, S. J. Perelman (from Jules Verne's novel), Photo; Lionel Linden, Mus; *Victor Young*. 178 minutes.
Oscars (4) Best Film, Best Screenplay (Poe, Farrow, Perelman), Best Photograph (Linden), Best Music (Young)

BARABBAS 1962 Columbia

Anthony Quinn (Barabbas), Silvana Mangano (Rachel), Arthur Kennedy (Pontius Pilate), Katy Jurado (Sara), Harry Andrews (Peter), Valentina Cortese (Julia), Vittoria Gassman (Sahak), *Jack Palance* (Torvald), Ernest Borgnine (Lucius).
Dir; *Richard Fleischer*. Prod; *Dino De Laurentiis*. Scr; *Christopher Fry*. Photo; *Aldo Tonti*. Mus; *Mario Nascimbene*. 139 minutes.

BATTLE OF THE BULGE 1966 Warner Bros.

Henry Fonda (Lt. Col. Kiley), *Robert Shaw* (Col. Hessler), Robert Ryan (Gen. Grey), Dana Andrews (Col. Pritchard), George Montgomery (Sgt. Duquesne), Ty Hardin (Lt. Schumacher), Pier Angeli (Louise), Barbara Werle (Elena), *Charles Bronson* (Wolemski), Werner Peters (Gen. Kohler), Hans Christian Blech (Conrad), James MacArthur (Lt. Weaver), *Telly Savalas* (Guffy).
Dir; *Ken Annakin*, Prod; *Milton Sperling, Philip Yordon*, Scr; Philip Yordon, Milton Sperling, John Melson, Photo; *Jack Hildyard*, Mus; Benjamin Frankel. 163 minutes.

BEN-HUR 1925 MGM

Ramon Novarro (Judah Ben-Hur), *Francis X. Bushman* (Messala), May McAvoy (Esther), Claire McDowell (Mother of Hur), Kathleen Key (Tirzah), Carmel Myers (Iras), Nigel de Brulier (Simonides), Mitchell Lewis (Sheik Ilderim), Leo White (Sanballat), Frank Currier (Quintus Arrius), Charles Belcher (Balthasar), Betty Bronson (Mary), Dale Fuller (Amrah), Winter Hall (Joseph).
Dir; *Fred Niblo*. Scr; June Mathis, Carey Wilson, Bess Meredith (Based on the novel by Lew Wallace). Photo; Rene Guissart, Karl Struss (race scenes) Percy Hilbum.

BEN-HUR 1959 MGM

Charlton Heston (Ben-Hur), Jack Hawkins (Quintus Arrius), *Stephen Boyd* (Messala), Haya Harareet (Esther), *Hugh Griffith* (Ilderim), Martha Scott (Miriam), *Sam Jaffe* (Simonides), Cathy O'Donnel (Tirzah), Finlay Currie (Balthasar), Frank Thring (Pilate). (Christ was portrayed by opera singer Claude Heater.)
Dir; *William Wyler*. Prod; *Sam Zimbalist*. Scr; *Karl Tunberg* (with additional scenes and dialogue by *Christopher Fry*) (based on the novel by Lew Wallace), Photo; *Robert Surtees*. Mus; *Miklos Rozsa*. 217 minutes.
Oscars (11) Best Picture. Best Director (Wyler), Best Actor (Heston), Best Supporting Actor (Griffith), Best Musical Score of a Dramatic Film (Rozsa), Best Film Editing (Ralph Winters, John Dunning), Best Sound (Franklin E. Milton), Best Special Effects (A. Arnold Gillespie, Robert MacDonald, Milo Lory), Best Colour Cinematography (Surtees), Best Colour Costume Design (Elizabeth Haffenden), Best Art Direction (William Horning, Edward Carfagno) *with* Best Set Decoration (Hugh Hunt).
Also nominated for Best Screenplay.

THE BIBLE . . . IN THE BEGINNING
1966 Twentieth Century Fox

Michael Parks (Adam), Ulla Bergryd (Eve), Richard Harris (Cain), *John Huston* (Noah), Stephen Boyd (Nimrod), *George C. Scott* (Abraham), Ava Gardner (Sarah), Peter O'Toole (Three Angels), Zoe Sallis (Hagar), Gabriele Ferzeti (Lot), Eleonora Rossi Drago (Lot's Wife), Franco Nero (Abel). Narrated by John Huston. Dir; *John Huston*. Prod; Dino De Laurentiis. Scr; Christopher Fry. Photo; *Giuseppe Rotunno*. Mus; Toshiro Mayuzumi. 175 minutes.

BIRTH OF A NATION 1915

Spottiswoode Aitken, Josephine Crowell, Henry B. Walthall, Andre Beranger, Miriam Cooper, Maxfield Stanley, Mae Marsh, Ralph Lewis, Lilliam Gish, Elmer Clifton, Robert Harron, Mary Alden.
Dir; *D. W. Griffith*. Ph; G. W. Bitzer. 165 minutes.

THE CHARGE OF THE LIGHT BRIGADE 1968 United Artists

Trevor Howard (Lord Cardigan), Vanessa Redgrave (Clarissa), *John Gielgud* (Lord Raglan), Harry Andrews (Lord Lucan), Jill Bennet (Mrs. Duberly), *David Hemmings* (Capt Nolan).
Prod/dir; *Tony Richardson*. Scr; *Charles Wood*. Photo; David Watkin, Neil Hartley. Mus; *John Addison*. 141 minutes.

EL CID 1961 Bronston-Dear Films

Charlton Heston (El Cid), *Sophia Loren* (Chimene), Raf Vallone (Ordonez), Genevieve Page (Urraca), *John Fraser* (Alfonso), Gary Raymond (Sancho), Hurd Hatfield (Arias), Massimo Serato (Fanez), Herbert Lom (Ben Yussuf), Frank Thring (Al Kadir), *Douglas Wilmer* (Moutamin), Michael Horden (Don Diego).
Dir; *Anthony Mann*. Prod; *Samuel Bronston*. Photo; *Robert Krasker*. Scr; *Frederic M. Frank, Philip Yordan*. Mus; *Miklos Rozsa*. 184 minutes.
Oscar Nominations; Best Song "The Falcon And The Dove" (Rozsa, Paul Francis Webster).

CLEOPATRA 1934 Paramount

Claudette Colbert (Cleopatra), Warren William (Julius Caesar), Henry Wilcoxon (Mark Antony), Joseph Schildkraut (Herod), Ian Keith (Octavian), C. Aubrey Smith (Enobarbus).
Dir; *Cecil B. DeMille*. Scr; Waldemar Young, Bartlett Comack, Vincent Lawrence. Photo; Victor Milner. 85 minutes.
Oscars (1) Best cinematography (Milner).

CLEOPATRA 1963 Twentieth Century Fox

Elizabeth Taylor (Cleopatra), *Richard Burton* (Antony), *Rex Harrison* (Caesar), Roddy McDowell (Octavian), Cesar Danova (Apollodorus), Hume Cronyn (Sosigenes),

Robert Stephens (Germnicus), Kenneth Haigh (Brutus), George Cole (Flavius), Martin Landau (Rufio), Andrew Keir (Agrippa), Isabelle Cooley (Charmian), Francesca Annis (Iris).
Dir; *Joseph L. Mankiewicz*. Prod; *Walter Wanger*. Scr; *Joe Mankiewicz*, Ranald MacDougall, Sidney Buchman. Photo; *Leon Shamroy*. Mus; Alex North. 243 minutes.
Oscars (4) Best Colour Cinematography (Shamroy), Best Colour Art Direction (Jack Martin Smith, Hilyard Brown, Herman Blumenthal, Elven Webb, Maurice Pelling, Boris Juraga) *with* Best Production Design (John De Cuir), Best Colour Costume Design (Irene Sharaff, Vittorio Nino Novarese, Renie), Best Special Effects (L. B. Abbott, Emil Kosa, Jr.).

CUSTER OF THE WEST 1967 ABC (Cinerama)

Robert Shaw (Custer), Mary Ure (Elizabeth Custer), Jeffrey Hunter (Lieut. Benteen), Ty Hardin (Major Reno), Charles Stalnaker (Lieut. Howells), Robert Hall (Sgt. Buckley), Lawrence Tierney (Gen. Sheridan), Kieron Moore (Cheyenne Chief), Marc Lawrence (Goldminer), *Robert Ryan* (Mulligan).
Dir; *Robert Siodmak*, Prod; Louis Dolivet, Philip Yordon, Scr; Bernard Gordon, Julian Halevy, Photo; *Cecilio Paniagua*, Mus; *Bernardo Segall*. 146 minutes.

DOCTOR ZHIVAGO 1965 MGM

Omar Sharif (Yuri Zhivago), Julie Christie (Lara), Geraldine Chaplin (Tonya), *Tom Courtenay* (Pasha), Alec Guinness (Yevgraf), Siobhan McKenna (Anna), Ralph Richardson (Alexander Gromeko), Rod Steiger (Komarovsky), Rita Tushingham (the Girl).
Dir; *David Lean*. Prod; Carlo Ponti. Scr; *Robert Bolt* (based on the book by Boris Pasternak), Photo; *Freddie A. Young*. Mus; *Maurice Jarre*. 197 minutes.
Oscars (5) Best Screenplay From Another Medium (Bolt), Best Colour Cinematography (Young), Best Colour Art Direction (Terence Marsh) *with* Best Set Decoration (John Box), Best Colour Costume Design (Phyllis Dalton), Best Music Score (Maurice Jarre).

THE FALL OF THE ROMAN EMPIRE 1964 Bronston

Sophia Loren (Lucilla), Stephen Boyd (Livius), *Alec Guiness* (Marcus Aurelius), *James Mason* (Timonides), *Christopher Plummer* (Commodus), Anthony Quale (Verulus), John Ireland (Ballomar), Mel Ferrer (Cleander), Omar Shariff (Sohamus), *Eric Porter* (Julianus), Douglas Wilmer (Niger).
Dir; *Anthony Mann*. Prod; *Samuel Bronston*. Scr; Ben Barzman, Basilio Franchina, Philip Yordan. Photo; *Robert Krasker*. Mus; *Dimitri Tiomkin*. 180 minutes.
Oscar Nomination; Best Music (Tiomkin).

55 DAYS AT PEKING 1963 Bronston

Charlton Heston (Major Matt Lewis), David Niven (Sir Arthur Robertson), Ava Gardner (Baroness Natalie Ivanhoff), Robert Helpmann (Prince Tuan), *Flora Robson* (Dowager Empress Tzu Hsi), Leo Genn (General Jung-Lu),

John Ireland (Sergeant Harry), Harry Andrews (Father de Bearn).
Dir; *Nicholas Ray* (taken over by *Guy Green* when Ray fell sick). Prod; *Samuel Bronston*. Scr; Philip Yordon, Bernard Gordon, Robert Hamer. Photo; *Jack Hildyard*. Mus; *Dimitri Tiomkin*. 154 minutes.
Oscar Nomination; Best Song "So Little Time" (Tiomkin, Paul Francis Webster).

GENGHIS KHAN 1965 Columbia

Stephen Boyd (Jamuga), *Omar Sharif* (Temujin-Genghis Khan), James Mason (Kam Ling), *Eli Wallach* (Shah of Khwarezm), *Francoise Dorleac* (Bortei), Telly Savalas (Shan), Robert Morley (Emperor of China), Yvonne Mitchell (Katke), Michael Horden (Geen), Woody Strode (Sengal), Kenneth Cope (Subodai).
Dir; *Henry Levin*, Prod; *Irving Allen*, Scr; *Clarke Reynolds, Beverly Cross*, Photo; Geoffrey Unsworth, mus; *Dusan Radic*. 126 minutes.

GONE WITH THE WIND 1939 Selznick/MGM

Vivien Leigh (Scarlett O'Hara), *Clark Gable* (Rhett Butler), *Leslie Howard* (Ashley Wilkes), Olivia de Havilland (Melanie), *Hattie McDaniel* (Mammy), Thomas Mitchell (Gerald O'Hara), Evelyn Keyes (Suellen O'Hara), Ann Rutherford (Carreen O'Hara), Butterfly McQueen (Prissy), Rand Brooks (Charles Hamilton), Laura Hope Crews (Aunt 'Pittypat' Hamilton), Harry Davenport (Dr. Meade), Ward Bond (Tom).
Dir; Victor Flemming (also George Cukor, Sam Woods and David O. Selznick. No one director is completely responsible for the excellence of this classic), Prod; *David O. Selznick*. Scr; Sidney Howard (based on the book by Margaret Mitchell). Photo; *Ernest Haller*. 220 minutes.
Oscars (9). Best film, Best Direction (Fleming), Best Actress (V. Leigh), Best Supporting Actress (H. McDaniel), Best Screenplay (Howard), Best Colour Cinematography (Haller), Best Art Direction (Lyle Wheeler), Best Editing (Hal C. Kern), Special Award to William Cameron Menzies (Sets) for outstanding achievement in the use of colour for the enhancement of dramatic mood.

GRAND PRIX 1966 MGM (Cinerama)

James Garner (Pete Aron), Eva Marie Saint (Louise Frederickson), *Yves Montand* (Jean-Pierre Sarti), Toshiro Mifune (Izo Yamura), Brian Bedford (Scott Stoddard), Jessica Walter (Pat).
Dir; *John Frankenheimer*. Acr; Robert Alan Parker. Photo; *Lionel Lindon*. Mus; Maurice Jarre. 175 minutes.
Oscars (3). Best Editing (Frederick Steinkamp, Henry Berman, Stewart Linder, Frank Santillo), Best Sound (Franklin Milton), Best Sound Effects (Gordon Daniel).

THE GREATEST STORY EVER TOLD 1964 United Artists (Cinerama)

Max Von Sydow (Jesus), Dorothy McQuire (Mary), Robert Loggia (Joseph), *Charlton Heston* (John the Baptist), *David McCallum* (Judas), Roddy McDowell (Matthew), John Constantine (John), *Gary Raymond* (Peter), Ina Balin (Martha of Bethany), Janet Margolin (Mary of Bethany), Sidney Poitier (Simone of Cyrene), *Joanna Dunham* (Mary Magdalene), Carroll Baker (Veronica), Pat Boone (Man at tomb), Van Heflin (Bar Amand), Sal Mineo (Uriah), Shelley Winters (Woman), John Wayne (Centurion), *Telly Savalas* (Pontius Pilate), Angela Lansbury (Claudia), *Jose Ferrer* (Herod Antipas), Claude Rains (Herod), Donald Pleasance (Dark Hermit), Richard Conte (Barabbas).
Dir/Prod; *George Stevens*, Scr; *James Lee Barrett, George Stevens* (based on Four Gospels, ancient writings and the book "The Greatest Story Ever Told" by *Fulton Oursler*, Photo; *William C. Mellor, Loyal Griggs*, Mus; *Alfred Newman*. 193 minutes.

THE GREAT RACE 1965 Warner Bros.

Jack Lemmon (Prof. Fate), *Tony Curtis* (The Great Leslie), *Natalie Wood* (Maggie DuBois), *Peter Falk* (Max), Keenan Wynn (Hezekiah), Arthur O'Connell (Henry Goodbody), Vivian Vance (Hester Goodbody), *Dorothy Provine* (Lily Olay), Larry Storch (Texas Jack), Ross Martin (Rolfe Von Stuppe).
Dir; *Blake Edwards*, Prod; *Martin Jurow*, Scr; *Arthur Ross*, Photo; *Russell Harlan*, Mus; Henry Mancini. 180 minutes.
Oscars (1) Best Sound Effects (Tregoweth Brown).

GUNS OF NAVARONE 1960 Columbia

Gregory Peck (Mallory), David Niven (Miller), *Anthony Quinn* (Andreas), Stanley Baker (Brown), Anthony Quale (Franklin), James Darren (Pappadimos), Irene Papas (Maria), Gia Scala (Anna), James Robertson Justice (Jensen), Richard Harris (Barnaby), Bryan Forbes (Cohn).
Dir; *J. Lee Thompson*, Producer; Cecil Ford, Executive Producer; Carl Foreman, Scr; Carl Foreman (based on the novel by Alistair MacLean), Mus; *Dimitri Tiomkin*, Photo; Oswald Morris. 157 minutes.
Oscars (1) Best Special Effects (Bill Warrington, visual; Vivian C. Greenham, audible).

THE HALLELUJAH TRAIL 1965 United Artists (Cinerama)

Burt Lancaster (Col Gearhart), Lee Remick (Cora Massingale), *Jim Hutton* (Captain Paul Slater), Pamela Tiffin (Louise), *Donald Pleasance* (Oracle Jones), *Brian Keith* (Frank Wallingham), *Martin Landeu* (Chief Walks-Stooped-Over), John Anderson (Sgt. Buell), Tom Stern (Kevin O'Flaherty).
Dir/Prod; *John Sturges*, Scr; John Gay (Based on the novel by Bill Gulick), Photo; *Robert Surtees*, Mus; *Elmer Bernstein*. 156 minute".

HOW THE WEST WAS WON 1962 MGM-Cinerama

Carroll Baker (Eve), Lee J. Cobb (Lew Ramsey), Henry Fonda (Jethro Stuart), Carolyn Jones (Julie Rawling), *Karl Malden* (Zebulon Prescott), *Gregory Peck* (Cleve Van Valen), *George Peppard* (Zeb Rawlings), Robert Preston (Roger Morgan), Debbie Reynolds (Lillith), *James Stewart* (Linus Rawlings), *Spencer Tracy* (the Narrator), Eli Wallach (Charley Gant), John Wayne (General Sherman), *Richard Widmark* (Mike King).

Dir; *Henry Hathaway*, John Ford, George Marshall, Prod; Bernard Smith, Scr; *James R. Webb*, Photo; William Daniels, Milton Krasner, Charles Lang Jr, Joseph LaShelle, Mus; *Alfred Newman*. 155 minutes.
Oscars (3) Best Story and Screenplay (James R. Webb), Best Editing (Harold F. Kress), Best Sound (Franklin Milton).

INTOLERANCE 1916

Lillian Gish, Mae Marsh, Fred Turner, Robert Harron, Sam de Grasse, Vera Lewis, Monte Blue, Tod Browning, Edward Dillon, Howard Gaye, Lillian Langdon, Olga Grey, Erich von Stroheim, Gunther von Rittau, Bessie Love, Margery Wilson, Eugene Pallette, Frank Bennett, Josephine Crowell, Constance Talmadge, Maxfield Stanley, Elmer Clifton, Alfred Paget, Seena Owen, Carl Stockdale, Tully Marshall, George Siegmann, Elmo Lincoln, Ted Duncan, Ruth St. Denis.
Dr; *D. W. Griffith*. Photo; *G. W. Bitzer, Karl Brown*. 183 minutes.

IT'S A MAD, MAD, MAD, MAD WORLD 1963 United Artists

Spencer Tracy (Capt. C. G. Culpeper), Milton Berle (J. Russell Finch), Sid Caesar (Melville Crump), Buddy Hackett (Benjy Benjamin), Ethel Merman (Mrs. Marcus), *Mickey Rooney* (Ding Bell), *Dick Shawn* (Sylvester Marcus), *Phil Silvers* (Otto Meyer), *Terry-Thomas* (J. Algernon Hawthorne), Jonathan Winters (Lennie Pike), Edie Adams (Monica Crump), Dorothy Provine (Emmeline Finch), Jimmy Durante (Smiler Grogan) guest stars include Peter Falk, Jim Bachus, Joe E. Brown, Andy Devine, Buster Keaton, The 3 Stooges, Jerry Lewis (unbilled).
Prod/Dir; *Stanley Kramer*, Scr; *William & Tania Rose*, Photo; Ernest Laszlo, Mus; Ernest Gold. 162 minutes.

JESUS OF NAZARETH 1975 ITC-RAI

Robert Powell (Jesus), Anne Bancroft (Mary Magdalene), Ernest Borgnine (Centurion), Claudia Cardinale (The Adulteress), Valentina Cortese (Herodias), James Farentino (Simon Peter), James Earl Jones (Balthazar), Stacy Keach (Barabbas), Tony Lo Bianco (Quintillius), James Mason (Joseph of Arimathea), Laurence Olivier (Nicodemus), Donald Pleasence (Melchior), *Anthony Quinn* (Caiaphas), Fernando Rey (Casper), Ralph Richardson (Simeon), Rod Steiger (Pontius Pilate), *Michael York* (John the Baptist), Ian Holm (Zerah), Olivia Hussey (Mary), *Ian McShane* (Judas), Yorgo Voyagis (Joseph), Norman Bowler (Saturninus), Cyril Cusack (Yehuda), Simon MacCorkindale (Roman), Oliver Tobias (Joel).
Dir; Franco Zeffirelli, Prod; *Vincenzo Labella*, Scr; Anthony Burgess, Suso Cecchi D'Amico, Franco Zeffirelli, Photo; *Armando Nannuzzi, David Watkin*, Music; *Maurice Jarre*.

JOAN THE WOMAN 1917 Paramount

Geraldine Farrar (Joan of Arc), Raymond Hatton (Charles III), Hobart Bosworth (General La Hire), Theodore Roberts (Cauchon), Wallace Reid (starving peasant), Ramon Novarro (starving peasant).

Dir/Prod; *Cecil B. DeMille*. Scr; Jeanie Macpherson. Photo; Alvin Wyckoff.

JULIUS CAESAR 1953 MGM

Marlon Brando (Mark Antony), *James Mason* (Brutus), *John Gielgud* (Cassius), Louis Calhern (Julius Caesar), Edmond O'Brien (Cada), Deborah Kerr (Portia), Greer Garson (Calpurnia), Richard Hale (Soothsayer), Alan Napier (Cicero).
Dir; *Joseph L. Mankiewicz*, Prod; Joseph Houseman, Screenplay Joseph L. Mankiewicz (from, of course, Shakespeare's play), Photo; Joseph Ruttenberg, Mus; *Miklos Rozsa*. 121 minutes.
Oscars (1) Best Black and White Art Direction (Cedric Gibbons, Edward Carfagno) *with* Best Set Decoration (Edwin B. Willis, Hugh Hunt).

JULIUS CAESAR 1969 Commonwealth United

Charlton Heston (Mark Antony), Jason Robards (Brutus), John Gielgud (Julius Caesar), *Richard Johnson* (Cassius), *Robert Vaughn* (Casca), Richard Chamberlain (Octavius Caesar), Diana Rigg (Portia), Christopher Lee (Artemidorus), Jill Bennett (Calpurnia).
Dir; Stuart Burge, Prod; *Peter Snell*, Scr; adapted by Robert Furnival, Photo; Ken Higgins, Mus; *Michael Lewis*. 116 minutes.

KHARTOUM 1966 United Artists (Cinerama)

Charlton Heston (General Gordon), *Laurence Olivier* (The Mahdi), Richard Johnson (Colonel J. D. H. Stewart), *Ralph Richardson* (Gladstone).
Dir; *Basil Dearden*, Prod; Juliun Blaustein, Scr; *Robert Ardrey*, Photo; *Ted Scarfe*, Mus; Frank Cordell. 128 minutes.
Oscar Nomination; Best Screenplay (Robert Ardrey).

KING OF KINGS 1927 Paramount

H. B. Warner (Jesus), Dorothy Cumming (Mary), Ernest Torrence (Peter), Joseph Schildkraut (Judas), Joseph Striker (John), *Jacqueline Logan* (Mary Magdalene).
Dir/Prod; *Cecil B. DeMille*. Scr; Jeanie Macpherson. Photo; Peverell Marley.

KING OF KINGS 1961 MGM-Bronston

Jeffrey Hunter (Jesus), Siobham McKenna (Mary), Hurd Hatfield (Pontius Pilate), *Ron Randell* (Lucius), Viveca Lindfors (Claudia), Rita Gam (Herodias), Carmen Sevilla (Mary Magdalene), *Brigid Bazlen* (Salome), *Harry Guardino* (Barabbas), *Rip Torn* (Judas), *Frank Thring* (Herod Antipas), Guy Rolfe (Caiphas), Robert Ryan (John the Baptist).
Dir; *Nicholas Ray*. Prod; *Samuel Bronston*, Scr; *Philip Yordon*, Photo; *Franz F. Planer, Milton Krasner, Manuel Berenguer*, Mus; *Miklos Rozsa*. 168 minutes.

LAWRENCE OF ARABIA 1962
Columbia/Horizon

Peter O'Toole (Lawrence), *Alec Guinness* (Prince Feisal), *Anthony Quinn* (Auda Abu Tayi), Jack Hawkins (General Allenby), *Jose Ferrer* (Turkish Bey), Anthony Quale (Col. Brighton), Claude Rains (Mr. Dryden), Arthur Kennedy (Jackson Bentley), Donald Wolfit (General Murray), *Omar Sharif* (Sherif Ali Ibn el Kharish).
Dir; *David Lean*, Prod; Sam Spiegel, Scr; *Robert Bolt*, Photo; *Freddie A. Young*, Mus; *Maurice Jarre*. 221 minutes.
Oscars (7) Best Film, Best Direction (Lean), Best Colour Photography (Young), Best Colour Art Design (John Box, John Stoll) *with* Best Set Decoration (Dario Simoni), Best Editing (Anne Coates), Best Sound Recording (John Cox), Best Original Music Score (Jarre).
Also nominated for Best Actor (O'Toole) and Best Supporting Actor (Sharif).

THE LONGEST DAY 1962 20th Century Fox

American—*John Wayne* (Lt. Col. Vandervoot), *Robert Mitchum* (Brig. Gen. Cota), *Henry Fonda* (Brig. Gen. Roosevelt), Robert Ryan (Brig. Gen. Gavin), Rod Steiger (Destroyer Commander), Robert Wagner (US Ranger), *Richard Beymer* (Pr. Schulz), Mel Ferrer (Maj. Gen. Haines), Jeffrey Hunter (Sgt. Fuller), Paul Anka (US Ranger), *Sal Mineo* (Pr. Martini), Edmund O'Brien (Gen. Barton), Roddy McDowall (Pr. Morris), Eddie Albert (Col. Newton), Red Buttons
British—Richard Burton (RAF Pilot), *Kenneth More* (Capt. Mand), Richard Todd (Maj. Howard), Peter Lawford (Lord Lovat), Leo Genn (Brig. Gen. Parker), John Gregson (Padre), Sean Connery (Pr. Flanagan), Michael Medwin (Pr. Watney), Patrick Barr (Gr. Capt. Stagg), Leslie Phillips (RAF Officer), Donald Houston (RAF Pilot), Frank Finlay (Pr. Coke), Lyndon Broke (Lt. Walsh), Bryan Coleman (Ronald Callan), Trevor Reid (Gen. Montgomery), Sian Phillips (Wren).
French—*Curt Jurgens* (Maj. Gen. Blumentutt), Werner Hins (F. M. Erwin Rommel), Paul Hartman (F. M. Gerd von Rundstedt), Gerd Froebe (Sgt. Kaffocklatsch), Hans Christian Blech (Maj. Werner Puskat).
Prod; *Darryl F. Zanuck*, Dir; (British) Ken Annakin, (American) Andrew Marton, (German) Bernard Wicki, Asst Prod; Elmo Williams, Scr; *Cornelius Ryan* (based on his book), Photo; Joan Bourgoin, Henri Porsin, Walter Wottitz, Mus; Maurice Jarre (Theme by Paul Anka). 180 minutes.
Oscars (2) Best Black and White Cinematography (Bourgoin, Wottitz, Porsin), Best Special Effects (Robert MacDonald, visual – Jacques Maumont, audible).
Also Nominated for Best Film.

MONTE CARLO OR BUST 1969
Paramount

Tony Curtis (Chester Schofield), Susan Hampshire (Betty), *Terry-Thomas* (Sir Cuthbert Ware-Armitage), Eric Sykes (Perkins), Gert Frobe (Schickel), Peer Schmidt (Otto), *Peter Cook* (Major Digby Dawlish), *Dudley Moore* (Lt. Kit Barrington).
Prod/Dir; *Ken Annakin*, Scr; *Jack Davies, Ken Annakin*, Photo; Gabor Pogany, Mus; Ron Goodwin. 125 minutes.

MUTINY ON THE BOUNTY 1962 MGM

Marlon Brando (Fletcher Christian), *Trevor Howard* (Captain Bligh), Richard Harris (John Mills), Hugh Griffith (Alexander Smith), Richard Hayden (William Brown), Percy Herbert (Mathew Quintal), Gordon Jackson (Edward Birkett), Noel Purcell (William McCoy), Tarita (Polynesian Girl), Chips Rafferty (Michael Byrne).
Dir; *Lewis Milestone*, Prod; *Aaron Rosenberg*, Scr; Charles Lederer (based on the book by Charles Nordhoff and James Norman Hale), Photo; *Robert L. Surtees*. 179 minutes.
Nominated for Best Film.

NOAH'S ARK 1928 Warner Bros.

Dolores Costello (Mary/Miriam), George O'Brien (Travis/Japhet), Malcolm White (Paul McAllister), Noah Beery (Nickoloff/King Nephilem), Louise Fazenda (Hilda/Tavern Maid), Guinn 'Big Boy' Williams (Al/Ham), Paul McAllister (Minister/Noah).
Dir; *Michael Curtiz*, Scr; Anthony Coldeway, Photo; Hal Mohr. 100 minutes.

QUO VADIS 1951 MGM

Robert Taylor (Marcus Vinicius), Deborah Kerr (Lygia), *Peter Ustinov* (Nero), *Leo Genn* (Petronius), *Finlay Currie* (Peter), Felix Aylmer (Plautius), Patricia Laffan (Poppaea).
Dir; *Mervyn LeRoy*, Prod; *Sam Zimbalist*, Scr; John Lee Mahin, Sonya Levien, S. N. Behrman (based on the book by Henryk Sienkiewicz), Photo; *Robert L. Surtees*, Mus; *Miklos Rozsa*. 171 minutes.

THE ROBE 1953 20th Century Fox

Richard Burton (Marcellus), Jean Simmons (Diana), Victor Mature (Demetrius), Michael Rennie (Peter), *Jay Robinson* (Caligula), Dean Jagger (Justus), Richard Boone (Pontius Pilate), Betta St John (Miriam), *Jeff Morrow* (Paulus).
Dir; Henry Koster, Scr; *Philip Dunne* (based on the novel by Lloyd C. Douglas), Photo; *Leon Shamroy*, Mus; *Alfred* Newman. 134 minutes.
Oscars (2) Best Colour Art Direction (Lyle Wheeler, George W. Davis) *with* Best Set Decoration (Walter M. Scott, Paul S. Fox), Best Colour Costume Design (Charles LeMaire, Emile Santiago).

SAMSON AND DELILAH 1950
Paramount

Victor Mature (Samson), Hedy Lamarr (Delilah), *George Sanders* (Saran of Gaza), Angela Lansbury (Semedar), Henry Wilcoxon (Ahtur), Olive Deering (Miriam), Fay Holden (Hazelponit), Julia Faye (Hisham), Russel Tamblyn (Saul), William Farnum (Tubal), Lane Chandler (Teresh).
Dir/Prod; *Cecil B. DeMille*, Scr; Jesse L. Lasky Jr., Frederick M. Frank, Photography; *George Barns*, Mus; Victor Young. 131 minutes.
Oscars (2) Best Colour Art Direction (Hans Dreier,

Walter Tyler) *with* Best Set Decoration (Sam Comer, Ray Moyer), Best Colour Costume Design (Edith Head, Dorothy Jenkins, Eloise Jenssen, Gile Steele, Gwen Wakeling).

SIGN OF THE CROSS 1932 Paramount

Frederick March (Marcus Superbus), Claudette Colbert (Poppaea), Elissa Landi (Mercia), Charles Laughton (Nero), Ian Keith (Tigellinus).
Dir/Prod; *Cecil B. DeMille*, Scr; Waldemar Young, Sidney Buchman. Photo; Karl Strauss, Mus; Rudolph Kopp. 105 minutes.

SODOM AND GOMORRAH 1962

Stewart Granger (Lot), *Pier Angeli* (Ildeth), *Stanley Baker* (Astaroth), Anouk Aimee (Bera), Rosanna Podesta (Shuah), Claudia Mori (Maleb), Rik Battaglia (Mechir), Giacomo Rossi Stuart (Ishmael), Feodor Chaliapin (Alabias), Enzo Fiermonte (Eber).
Dir; Robert Aldrich, Prod; Geoffredo Lombardo, Scr; Hugo Butler, Giorgio Prosperi, Photo; Silvano Ippoliti, Marior Montuori, Cyril Knowles, Leonardo Bedini, Aldo De Robertis, Mus; *Miklos Rozsa*. 123 minutes.

SOLOMON AND SHEBA 1959 United Artists

Yul Brynner (Solomon), Gina Lollobrigida (Queen of Sheba), George Sanders (Adonijah), Marisa Pavan (Abishag), John Crawford (Joab), Laurence Naismith (Hezrai), Harry Andrews (Baltor), Finlay Currie (King David), David Farrar (Pharoah), William Devlin (Nathan), Jean Anderson (Takyan), Jack Gwillim (Josiah).
Dir; King Vidor, Prod; Ted Richmond, Scr; Anthony Veiller, Paul Dudley, George Bruce, Photo; *Freddie Young*, Mus; Mario Nascimbene. 139 minutes.

SPARTACUS 1960 Universal/Bryna

Kirk Douglas (Spartacus), *Laurence Olivier* (Crassus), Jean Simmons (Varinia), *Charles Laughton* (Gracchus), *Peter Ustinov* (Batiatus), John Gavin (Julius Caesar), Tony Curtis (Antoninus), Nina Foch (Helena), John Dall (Glabrus), Charles McGraw (Marcellus), Joanna Barnes (Claudia), Harold J. Stone (David), Woody Strode (Draba).
Dir; *Stanley Kubrick*, prod; Edward Lewis, Exec Prod; *Kirk Douglas*, Scr; *Dalton Trumbo* (based on the novel by Howard Fast), Photo; *Russel Metty*, Mus; *Alex North*. 193 minutes.
Oscars (4) Best Supporting Actor (Ustinov), Best Colour Cinematography (Metty), Best Colour Art Direction (Eric Orbom) *with* Best Set Decoration (Russell A. Gausman, Julia Heron), Best Colour Costume Design (Valles, Peruzzi, Bill Thomas).

TARAS BULBA 1962 United Artists

Tony Curtis (Andrei), *Yul Brynner* (Taras Bulba), Christine Kaufman (Natalia), Sam Wanamaker (Filipenko), Brad Bexter (Shilo), Guy Rolfe (Prince Grigory), *Perry Lopez* (Ostap), Ilka Windish (Mother of the Brothers Bulba), Stepan (Vladmir Sokoloff).
ir; *J. Lee Thompson*, Prod; *Harold Hecht*, Scr; *Waldo

Salt, *Karl Tunberg* (based on the novel by Nikolai Gogol), Photo; Joe MacDonald. Mus; *Franz Waxman*. 122 minutes.
Oscar Nomination; Best Music (Waxman).

THE TEN COMMANDMENTS 1923 Paramount

Part One—Theodore Roberts (Moses), Charles De Roche (Rameses), Estelle Taylor (Miriam), Part Two—Edythe Chapman (Mrs Martha McTavish), Richard Dix (John McTavish), Rod La Rocque (Dan McTavish), Leatrice Joy (Mary Leigh).
Dir/Prod; *Cecil B. DeMille*, Scr; Jeanie Macpherson, Photo; Bert Glennon.

THE TEN COMMANDMENTS 1956 Paramount

Charlton Heston (Moses), *Yul Brynner* (Rameses), Anne Baxter (Nefretiri), *Edward G. Robinson* (Dathan), Debra Paget (Lilia), Yvonne De Carlo (Sephora), John Derek (Joshua), *Sir Cedric Hardwicke* (Seth), Nina Foch (Bithiah), Martha Scott (Yochabel), Judith Anderson (Memnet), Vincent Price (Baka).
Dir/Prod; *Cecil B. DeMille*, Scr; *Aeneas MacKenzie, Jesse L. Lasky Jr., Jack Gariss, Frederick M. Frank*, Photo; *Loyal Griggs*, Mus; *Elmer Bernstein*. 221 minutes.
Oscars (1) Best Special Effects (John Fulton).

2001: A SPACE ODYSSEY 1969 MGM (Cinerama)

Keir Dullea (Bowman), Gary Lockwood (Poole), Douglas Rain (Voice of HAL), William Sylvester, Leonard Rossiter, Margaret Tyzack, Robert Beatty.
Dir/Prod; *Stanley Kubrick*, Scr; *Stanley Kubrick, Arthur C. Clarke*, Photo; *Geoffrey Unsworth*. 141 minutes.
Oscars (1) Best Special Visual Effects (Stanley Kubrick).

THE VIKINGS 1958 United Artists/ Bryna

Kirk Douglas (Einar), *Tony Curtis* (Eric), Ernest Borgnine (Ragnar), Janet Leigh (Morgana), James Donald (Egbert).
Dir; Richard Fleischer, Scr; Calder Willingham, Photo; *Jack Cardiff*, Mus; Mario Nascimbene. 112 minutes.

WAR AND PEACE 1956 Paramount

Audrey Hepburn (Natasha), Henry Fonda (Pierre Bezukhov), Mel Ferrer (Prince Audrey), Vittorio Gassman (Anatole Kuragin), Herbert Lom (Napoleon), Oscar Homolka (Gen. Kutuzov), Anita Ekberg (Helene), Jeremy Brett (Nicholas Rostov), May Britt (Sonya Rostov), Wilfred Lawson (Prince Bolkonsky), Sean Barrett (Petya Rostov), John Mills (Platon Karatsev).
Dir; *King Vidor*, Prod; Dino De Laurentiis, Scr; Bridget Boland, Robert Westerby, King Vidor, Mario Camerini, Ennio de Concini, Ivo Perilli (from the novel by Leo Tolsboy), Photo; *Jack Cardiff*, Mus; Nino Rota. 178 minutes.

WAR AND PEACE 1963 Mosfilm

Ludmilla Savelyeva (Natasha), Sergei Bondarchuk (Pierre), Vyacheslav Tihonov (Andrei Bolkonsky), Victor Stanitsin (Count Rostov).
Dir; *Sergei Bondarchuk*, Scr; *Sergei Bondarchuk, Vasily Solovyov* (from the novel by Leo Tolsboy), Photo; *Anatoly Petrisky*, Mus; *Vyacheslav Ovchinnikov*. 455 minutes.
Oscars (1) Best Foreign Language Film.

THE WAR LORD Universal 1965

Charlton Heston (Chrysagon), Richard Boone (Bors), Rosemary Forsyth (Bronwyn), Maurice Evans (Priest), *Guy Stockwell* (Draco), Niall MacGinnis (Odins), Henry Wilcoxon (Frisian Prince), James Farentino (Marc).
Dir; *Franklin Schaffner*, Prod; Walter Seltzer, Scr; *John Collier, Millard Kaufman* (based on the play "The Lovers" by Leslie Stevens), Photo; *Russell Metty*, Mus; *Jerome Moross*. 123 minutes.

WATERLOO 1970 Columbia

Rod Steiger (Napoleon), Christopher Plummer (Wellington), Orson Welles (Louis XVIII), Jack Hawkins (Gen. Picton), Virginia McKenna (Duchess of Richmond), Dan O'Herlihy (Marshall Ney), Rupert Davies (Gordon).
Dir; *Sergie Bondarchuk*, Prod; *Dino De Laurentiis*, Scr; H. A. L. Craig, Sergei Bondarchuk, Vittorio Bonicelli, Mus; Nino Rota. 132 minutes.

ZULU 1963 Paramount-Diamond-Embassy

Stanley Baker (Lt. John Chard), Jack Hawkins (Rev. Otto Witt), Ulla Jacobson (Margareta Witt), *James Booth* (Pr. Henry Hook), *Michael Caine* (Lt. Bromhead), *Nigel Green* (Colour-Sgt Bourne).
Dir; *Cy Enfield*, Prod; *Stanley Baker, Cy Enfield*, Scr; *John Prebble, Cy Enfield*, Photo; *Stephen Dabe*, Mus; *John Barry*. 135 minutes.

ELDER PARK LIBRARY